A GUIDE TO CRICUT: THE ART OF THE MACHINE

By Tracey Clapp

legal, financial, medical or professional advice. The content within this book has been derived from various sources.

By reading this document, the reader agrees that under no circumstances are is the author responsible for any losses, direct or indirect, which are incurred because of the use of information contained within this document, including, but not limited to, —errors, omissions, or inaccuracies.

Contents

Introduction

What is the Cricut Maker and why do so many people want this machine? This guide has been created to help the beginner and even the novice or, indeed, expert learn more about the Cricut Maker and understand all the components involved in this interesting machine. There are literally thousands of various projects people can create using the Cricut Maker.

Quite simply, the Cricut Maker cuts hundreds of materials quickly and accurately, from the most delicate paper and fabric to matboard and leather. There is an expandable collection of tools to use with the included powerful blade rotary blade. Also included are pens and scoring tools. The Cricut Maker grows with the user as new crafts and techniques are learned.

The name Cricut comes from the actual name brand of the Cricut Maker. The Cricut is a sewing and craft-making machine that literally cuts down hours and steps from crafting projects and helps even the novice crafter create projects that look professionally finished.

The original Cricut machine was basically used for scrapbooking and cutting paper and card stock. People were amazed at the ease at which this made various other crafting projects as well.

The Cricut Maker that people are purchasing today can design and cut almost anything you can imagine. The Cricut Maker is not just a paper cutter but specializes in designing and cutting vinyl, leather, lighter wood types, and so much more. Whatever you can imagine, the Cricut Maker can do.

The new rotary blade that comes with the Cricut Maker is said to cut material and most types of cloth-like butter! And the pen can mark the patterns and then cut them for you. Cricut Maker has partnered up with Simplicity and now makes several patterns available through Design Space.

In this guide, we will cover the Cricut Maker Machine and its components. We will also talk about the accessories you can buy and which ones you should buy based on how much you use your Cricut Maker. We will also introduce the reader to several basic projects the Cricut Maker can make and will then get into some more advanced projects as well. Then, we will also look at some unique but fairly easy projects you can make as a new Cricut Maker user.

The program, Design Space, will be discussed in depth throughout this guide, and you will get a good idea as to why this is a real asset to you as a Cricut Maker crafter. Design Space enables most of your projects to be created with greater ease and with professional style.

This guide will also give you a great look at all the available accessories and what they are used for in various projects. You will know what to do and when with each accessory after reading this guide. You will also have a complete list of the different vocabulary words and the definitions of each word.

As you become more familiar with your machine and people start seeing what you can create, friends and relatives may start asking for special projects, or want to order copies of various things that they've seen you do. The idea of going into business with your Cricut may be on your mind. This Guide has devoted an entire chapter about how to start a business with your Cricut Maker including facts about licensing and taxes.

You will learn the steps of how to decide if going into business is for you or if you want to keep crafting a hobby. But either way, you will enjoy reading this guide from beginning to end.

You will also learn how to troubleshoot problems, should you have any with your Cricut Maker, and you will also learn how to keep your Cricut Maker in the best possible working order so to avoid unnecessary repairs with your machine.

The Cricut Maker is almost infallible, as you will find out if you purchase one and there is help at the click of a button.

Did you know the Cricut Maker can even charge your phone? Yes, this machine even charges your phone. This Cricut Maker is designed to keep you working at your craft table and busy without interruptions for a reason. The manufacturers know that people who are serious crafters really want to keep crafting. It was previously mentioned that the Cricut Maker enables sewing projects to become easier. As you will see in our sewing chapter, the Cricut Maker literally marks and cuts patterns. Cricut has a partnership with Simplicity. One user said after receiving her Cricut Maker, "The more I learn about my Cricut maker, the better I like it and the more confident I become!" Like almost every other Cricut user who seems thrilled with their new machine, this user also loved how much easier sewing and other crafts were after using the new Cricut Maker.

This Cricut owner is correct. Having a new machine is the beginning. The fun comes from getting to know your machine and learning about everything you can do. There are endless amounts of techniques to learn when using your Cricut Maker. But for now, let's begin by doing one thing at a time. Grab your favorite beverage and just enjoy unpacking your new Cricut Maker.

Another Cricut owner was simply gushing when she opened her Cricut Maker box. "I have never been so excited about a gift before in my life. This is just a dream! I have been pinning different things on Pinterest that I want to try, but I hear some projects are already included with the new machines. I just love the color!"

Yet another new Cricut Maker owner also said, "I had my craft room all set up and I have been blogging for a while. One of the people who follow me asked me if I was ever going to get a Cricut machine. When my husband surprised me with the new Cricut Maker, I could not believe it! I plan to set up and get going this evening."

Finally, one user said, "We converted an entire section of our basement for crafts. My wife and I both enjoy crafts. I do wood crafts and I'm hoping with the new Cricut Maker, we can print sayings in vinyl for the wood. We already have a sign business but think this Cricut Maker will take us to the next level. People have told us the efficiency and time saved when using the machine will help us reduce our hours and of course increase the fun while working together on our project."

Chapter 1

Cricut Maker Machines and their components

There have been numerous different kinds of Cricut machines manufactured since the first Cricut was made in 2006. The Cricut Maker has completely changed the crafting world for many individuals who craft for fun and who make crafts for a living. Since its inception, there have been several different models and various different features with each new model released. Almost every year, since 2011, a new Cricut has been released with even more capabilities than the ones previously.

Several current models are being used today.

The Cricut Explore One is a lot like the original Cricut but has evolved into a die cutting machine. Not only does it cut paper, but it also cuts other materials such as fabric to name a few.

Other similar models include the **Explore Air**, the **Cricut Explore Air 2**, and the **Cricut Maker**. There are legacy machines and machines that are retired, but in this guide, we are going to focus primarily on the Cricut Maker, the components of the Cricut Maker and how to use the Cricut Maker.

The Components of a Cricut Maker

The Cricut maker is going to come with a few components necessary to start making basic projects. They are:

- A rotary blade
- A fine point blade with housing
- A Cricut brand fine point pen
- Two connecting cords
- A manual

There are many other accessories you may want to buy as you get to know your machine and start making projects. And this guide will outline which of these you may want to purchase next for certain projects in later chapters.

Unpacking Your Machine

1. Take your time to open the Cricut Maker. Find a long table with plenty of space to open the box and look at everything.

2. In the box, you will find your machine, the above-listed components and the box. It is recommended to keep the box just in case you want to take your Cricut Maker to a friend's house, a craft fair, crafting retreat, or even resale it to purchase a newer model.

3. The two cords, as mentioned above, have two uses. One cord is for plugging the machine into an outlet and the other cord is for hooking your machine up to your laptop.

Does the Cricut Maker Use Cartridges?

The newer Cricut Maker no longer uses Cartridges. These machines are designed to be used with a laptop computer. So, if someone mentions cartridges to you, you can reply with the knowledge that your Cricut Maker does not need a cartridge.

If I have older cartridges, can I still use them with my newer machine?

Yes! You can definitely use all of your old cartridges with any of the electronic Cricut machines. The legacy is no longer sold by Cricut. But the Expression series can use the cartridges as they always have by physically inserting them into the machine and using the keyboard overlay or connecting them to the Cricut Craft Room to edit on a computer.

Even the newest machines, the Cricut Explore series and the Cricut Maker, can still use any cartridges you have purchased from Cricut. You first have to link them to your Cricut account so you can access them online through Cricut Design Space.

The **rotary blade** listed above is the blade component that comes with your Cricut maker. This blade is precise and accurate. It is almost like a handheld X-ACTO knife blade people used to use for precision cuts, but so much more accurate. One person who has essential tremor, (this is a disease that causes shakiness in hands and voice), said, "I used to love crafting and sewing, but I had to stop because I would shake so bad. Now with my Cricut Maker, I am able to make more precise cuts than ever before and crafting is fun again."

The rotary blade that comes with your machine allows you to cut material as fine as crepe paper up to materials as thick as leather.

There are more blades you may want to purchase once you start using the machine and get into even more advanced projects. There are seven types of blades to use with the Cricut machine.

The **fine point blade with housing** that is included with your Cricut maker is used to make the most detailed cuts on materials such as poster board, card stock, paper, etc. The materials should not be very heavyweight. This is for more detail-oriented projects.

A **fine point pen** is the last component included with your Cricut Maker. Your Cricut machine has two clips at the front. Clamp A and Clamp B. Open clamp A and that is how you insert your pen after you remove the lid. To test the fine point pen, put it in the clamp and then go into your writing fonts and choose a font. You should have a white paper underneath the pen to experiment. You decide what you are going to write in Design Space and then press "Go".

Your Cricut Maker is not just for cutting but is an excellent tool for writing as well. There are so many uses for this writing tool. People address envelopes, write letters, do calligraphy, and make their own sign designs using their pens. The Cricut will use other pens beside just the Cricut pens. And depending on which design you might be doing using Design Space, the program will tell you the size and color of the pens to use. You can turn any picture or graphic into a drawing with this tool.

Chapter 2

Nuts and Bolts – How does The Cricut Maker Work?

The Cricut Maker is made so that there are applications and tools to make almost any crafting project possible. In order to do those projects, it is important for the user to understand what is involved in those applications, which ones are free, how much some cost, and what is needed for each project for the machine to work. We will first look at some of the applications used in the Cricut Maker.

Design Space and Cricut Access

Design Space is the FREE software for uploading your projects, refining them and sending to your Cricut Machine.

Cricut Access is the paid membership. It contains graphics, fonts and projects to be used within Cricut Design Space. Cricut Access is possibly one of the best purchases to make after you obtain a Cricut Maker. Cricut Access has a cost of $95.80 per year or you can set up payments for $9.99 per month. This application literally has hundreds of uses and opens up a whole world of over 1000 projects and hundreds of fonts.

So many crafts are used with Design Space and Cricut Access. It is worth pointing out at this stage that you can use your Cricut Maker without Cricut Access. It shows very clearly in Design Space what is chargeable and what isn't and you can make the choice accordingly.

This Guide does not try to sell products, but Cricut Access is recommended with the Cricut Maker, especially if you use your Cricut Maker as part of your business. Cricut Access offers so much in the way of processing applications from files to your Cricut Maker. The price per month or the money per year is small compared to the benefits you will get from it. The alternative to Cricut Access Membership is pay as you go, which soon adds up. So, it is a worthwhile purchase.

SnapMat

SnapMat is an exclusive feature for the iOS version of Design Space. With SnapMat you can capture a photo of your material on the cutting mat so you know exactly where your image will be cut. Brilliant! Not only does this help you put your image exactly where you want it, but it also helps you use up scraps of paper and fabric with less waste!

SnapMat takes the guessing out of image placement on the mat preview by showing you where your text and images will be cut or drawn. With SnapMat, you can cut around a specific location of a photo, pattern, or stamped page. You can also write in specific locations on envelopes, greeting cards, or gift tags. And you can also use scrap materials with greater confidence and less waste of materials.

Inkscape

Inkscape is not specifically made for Cricut users but it is a great graphics editor for making SVG files out of regular JPEG images. It's a completely free software for all the major desktop operating systems so you can easily download it, install it and open your JPEG image. From there, you just have to make a bitmap copy and then move the bitmap copy over so you can see the first image. Select the first image and delete it. Now you can put your bitmap image onto your canvas. This is a great way to import images to your Cricut Maker.

Images

SVG files are what is mostly used with the Cricut Maker. This allows you to make more precise cuts than a JPG or PNG file.

These SVG files are downloaded from the web and are used to create different designs. There are several websites where SVG files are available for a reasonable cost. They feature various fonts, graphics, and often offer the commercial licenses included in the price of the files as a bonus. If you sell your items, the licenses to do so are already included in your products.

If your download comes in a ZIP file, you will need to make sure to extract your SVG before uploading. You cannot upload a ZIP file to Cricut Design Space.

Navigate through the examples and choose the file you want to use. Click Save. The file should appear in your recently uploaded images. Select it and click insert images and your chosen file will import onto your canvas.

You can make projects using your own photos and designs. The Cricut Maker has a variety of tools to use in conjunction with your computer to make different personalized projects. Inkspace is completely optional as you can also upload personalized images using Cricut Design Space and then make the cuts using your machine.

Uploading Your Own Images on Design Space

The ability to upload your own images gives you so much freedom to create anything you want with your Cricut Maker. You can upload anything from basic, flat jpeg images to advanced, multi-layer vector files and Cricut Design Space will automatically process them so you can print, emboss, cut, or use them however you want in your Cricut project!

To upload any image in your Design Space, you must first open your Cricut Design Space on your computer. When you locate the green button that says, "new project," please click that button. It should be in the upper right-hand corner of the screen. This will create a new project. Now, look at the toolbar. At the bottom of the bar on the left-hand side is an upload button or icon. Click that icon. For example, something as simple as a graphic in Adobe Illustrator then saves it as both a jpg and an SVG file so you can upload a basic image and a vector image to Cricut Design Space. Any file will work, but this would be a great test run.

Many of the images you see on the internet are 2D images. They are called basic images. These images can have more than one color and can even look multi-dimensional, but the photo or image is a single layer. It just looks like it has more depth than it actually does. All of these single-layer images can be created in various programs like Photoshop, Canva, Adobe, and others. Another example of 2D images are photos from your phone. Camera photos are also basic images.

The Cricut Maker can give you hours of fun as you work with uploaded 2D images. They can be in various files in the Cricut design space and will all come as a single layer file. When you upload a basic image in Cricut Design Space, you will have the program open and then will click on the white and green upload image tab.

You will then drag and drop the image into the window. Or browse to find the image. After you choose a basic image to upload, you will get a preview and then you will select images to make choices from.

Simple images are very basic images with contrasting colors with a solid background.

Moderately complex Images are images with more details and more colors. There is still more contrast between the colors, but maybe not as significant. You can still tell the difference between the image and the background.

Complex Images are detailed images with blended colors and it is difficult to tell the difference between the background and foreground. There are varying levels of shading and blending.

When you are working with images and your Cricut, the next step after you upload image is to process the image. You need to make sure the parts of the image that you want to cut out with your Cricut Maker are the parts you are going to process. You may use the following tools to work with your image to help get the exact selections you want.

- **Select and Erase** – This is a typical erase button much like in your MacBook erase button if you have one. This helps you to choose an area or even a color in your image and erase it. There is also an advanced option to allow you to change the tolerance of what you erase.
- **Erase** – This is just a regular eraser. The eraser can change the size by sliding to the left.
- **Crop** – This is used for what it says, to crop an image.

Most Cricut Maker crafters use "Select & Erase" for about 90% of the images they upload onto Cricut Design Space.

They say, "it's really powerful and really smart!" You can erase things like the background and highlight people or pets, for instance.

Now, you need to choose the kind of image you have and label the image. You can save the image as a Cut Image or as a Print and Cut Image. You have to decide how you want to save it. Mostly it depends on how much you want to cut. After you give the image a name, click "Save."

The easy locator for the image is that now your uploaded image will appear in the "recently uploaded images" section so that now it can be located quickly. Just select the image and insert this image into your project!

Uploading Vector Images in Design Space

Vector images are image files that involve more than a single layer. They are usually created in a design program such as Adobe Illustrator. You can also upload these kinds of files to Cricut Design Space and the files will upload as individual layers or several layers meshed together as one.

As a rule, Vector images are files with more than one layer. They are usually created in a program as mentioned above, like Adobe Illustrator. You can upload DXF and SVG files to Cricut Design Space and they will be uploaded as several layers with their own image layer or color then separating out. You will then be able to see the separate layers in Design Space.

To Upload a vector image in Cricut Design Space, click the upload image button. This button is green in Design Space. You can then click on the image or drag and drop the image file into the window. Of course, you can always browse images and then click on the choice of the image you have named, and it will upload.

Vector image files have all of the details an image needs within the file itself. The Cricut Maker is so versatile it actually is able to process these image files for you automatically. The Cricut Maker gives you a preview of the image on the left-hand side and after each layer has actually uploaded and every color, you will just give the image a name and save the image.

This is much like our previous explanation of uploading your own images. You will select the recent image from the recently uploaded images section. Then you will insert the image onto your canvas. The vector image will appear with all of its colors. The basic image will still be in the one single layer on the right side of the screen and the vector image will be on the left side of the screen and will be split into the layers or the colors.

When using Cricut Design Space, the language referring to layers actually means colors. When a design is cut, the Cricut Maker will automatically split the various colors into different cuts, so they are cut out of different materials if that is what you wish to do.

If the SVG file you upload is all one color, Cricut Design Space will automatically split each layer into different and separate layers for your project. Vector images are more useful if you are planning to cut from different materials or different colors because the colors will automatically change into the layers you will be cutting in Cricut Design Space. And, for a simple cut or Print & Cut projects, uploading a basic image will work just great.

How to do a Test Cut

To make a test cut, do some simple shapes to do your test cut with. Insert a rectangle or another shape to see if your material and your blade are correct. More often than not, the Cricut Maker will tell you if the blade or the mat is incorrect. Follow the directions.

The test cut does not have to be big — the top right-hand corner of vinyl or material. Size the shape down and you are ready to make your cut. Send it to your Cricut Maker and load the vinyl or whatever material and cut it. Again, it's not going to use very much at all. If the cut is successful, you are ready to go. If there is a problem, turn to our troubleshooting chapter, Chapter 9.

Writing and Drawing with the Cricut Maker

If you love to write or draw, you can create hand-drawn accents on many of your projects. This might include personal illustrations or coloring page designs. This works even if you are not comfortable drawing this art yourself. The Cricut Maker will do many of these projects for you.

Almost any cut design can have drawing elements added to it. You can experiment with the designs to see what looks good with the drawing elements added in. Look at your cut files and convert those into drawing designs. Look carefully at the screen, because what you see on the screen is what is going to print.

To create a drawing or writing line in Cricut Design Space, simply make the lines to say "writing." Follow these steps:

Select the image you want to draw. Click on the layer or the icon of the image. Then your palette will open and will allow you to select "writing" for this layer. Then you choose your pen color for that layer of your image.

And, at the same time, you can choose the same color on your screen so you can preview how this will look. Make sure you are choosing the same color with the same pen.

When your Cricut Maker is working, it will cue you as to when to change pen colors as needed. For all the colors you selected on the screen, the Design Space will call for those colors as it is creating the design. You will notice after playing with this function on your Cricut Maker that almost any image can be made into a drawing.

More Drawing Tips

When you are drawing and you want to keep a layout together, you should attach the drawing lines together. This action will not assist you in a specific layout, but it will let you move pieces of the drawing together around on the canvas.

Attach the drawing to your canvas layout. If you are working with a specific shape, try to remember to attach the drawing to the cut design. If you do this several times, it will become automatic.

Now you can cut the design and the drawing making sure the drawing is attached to the cut design.

If you do not have a specific cut design that you want to attach to the drawing, you can move the drawing around on the final mat view of this. Make sure to place your paper on the mat in coordination with where you believe the drawing will appear.

Again, you should pay close attention as to how the lines look on the screen. How lines appear on the computer screen is how they will appear on your printed surface. If designs are overlapping on the screen, they will overlap in the printing.

Test the different pen types. Try the different names and colors and also how different inks look on the different texture of papers. Gold glitter isn't nearly as bold as gold metallic. You will see as you look at different pens and colors which colors you prefer and also which textures of papers you prefer with certain colors.

Tips and Tricks when using your Cricut Maker:

1. **Place your Cricut Make on a long table.** This will give you plenty of room for all of your materials and your computer. More room equals less frustration. You will also be able to keep your materials neater if you have plenty of room and space. We cannot emphasize this enough. You need room to work and room to have materials and organization.

2. **Install the Cricut Design Space Software.** It is a great idea to install it on both your laptop and your iPhone. If you have it on both devices, you can follow along on your iPhone when your laptop is talking to your Cricut. You need Design Space. And having it on at least two devices is a great idea.

3. **Your first project should be on the easier side.** It is very easy to be intimidated with this new machine. But don't let it sit in the box. Unpack it as this guide instructed you and start with a small project. The best way to learn how to do something is by actually

doing it. We can give you instructions, but until you actually get in there and get some experience, this will not mean as much until you do. Then you'll reread this and go, "Oh yes. I get it now." There are tons of videos out there to watch as well. Watch them before and after you try a few things.

There are ready-to-make projects you can choose with card stock. Choose one of those so you can get familiar with your cutting machine. Open the Cricut Design Space on your computer. You can make your own project or choose a "Make it Now" project. These projects are designed to be completed from beginning to end and are simple for a beginner. This is highly recommended to get the basics down and to avoid frustration. This will help you become more used to the tools of your Cricut Maker.

The machine will even tell you when to change materials and change blades. It will also help select mats on these beginning projects. These introductory projects are there for a very good reason. Plus, they are great projects!

4. **Peel the mats away from paper, card stock, etc.**
   This trick is actually on one of the Cricut video tutorials, but it is a great tip! When you peel away the mat from the paper, it comes off nicely. However, when you peel the paper off the mat, the paper often curls. This is completely frustrating. It's

no fun to be frustrated with something as simple as paper curling up. This is a great tip to keep that from happening.

5. **Use a spatula to carefully lift the intricate designs off the mat.** This step will prevent the designs from tearing. Don't get upset if your design has a slight rip. You can usually make it almost invisible when you put it on the finalized piece. This is such a simple tool and method to keep your designs in one piece.

6. **You can use the "customize" option to make changes to an existing Cricut design.** You can add to any design to make it your own. Once you get more confident with your Cricut Maker, you can even change the "Make it Now" projects. You can add details, change the fonts, sizes, and more.

7. **Have a simple set of tools ready.** The weeder, spatula, scraper and tweezers are so handy for lifting up vinyl and detailed paper designs, applying transfer tape, and cleaning scraps off the mat. You should have these at the ready. There is nothing more frustrating than needing a tool and having to look for it. Remember Christmas and wrapping gifts? Have you ever lost your tape or scissors or laid them under the paper? This is so annoying. Keep

your tools where you can see them and also your work area neat. Some people actually make a tool caddie that attaches to their Cricut Maker and has a place for the essential tools they will need. This way they always have their essential tools.

8. **Use cheat sheets and videos.** There are so many Cricut "expert" bloggers sharing their free Cricut cheat sheets to make things easier for everyone. Have them handy as quick references! If you go to Pinterest and search "Cricut cheat Sheets" numerous walls will pop up. Not just two or three, but 50 or more people have cheat sheets to offer!

9. **Let Cricut prompts guide you.** The Cricut Maker is impressive. it guides you through every step from selecting materials to loading mats to using the right blades. There are prompts telling you to push certain buttons and load different blades. Listen to your Cricut Maker.

10. **Use the test cut feature**. There is a test cut feature in your Cricut Maker. It is featured in this Guidebook just before this section on Tips and Tricks.

11. **Keep your crafting space neat and organized.** Sometimes this is difficult, but you will enjoy crafting and will have more success if you have a

more organized space in which to do all of your Cricut Maker crafts. We cannot stress this often enough. Being neat is a great habit to get into when using your Cricut Maker.

The Cricut Maker Cuts Materials

The Cricut Maker is able to cut a number of materials, which is what makes this machine the powerhouse of crafting tools. Actually, there are over 100 different materials the Cricut Maker is able to cut. This is not just for cutting paper and vinyl. This machine can be used for so much more.

However, the beginner should start with paper, vinyl, fabric, or some type of iron-on material. These are the **basic four materials** to learn to cut with your Cricut Maker.

Vinyl

The first one is vinyl. Vinyl is what you use to add your touch to many of the projects you use the Cricut maker for such as personalized objects, mugs, glasses, bags and more.

For people just getting started, there is a Cricut Vinyl Sampler available for purchase, which comes with twelve 12" x 12" sheets of adhesive vinyl in a variety of colors. There's also a metallic vinyl sampler you want to try some fun metallics for your project. Either selection will get you started, and if you end up loving vinyl, there are many projects you can try.

Fabric

You really should get some fabric and try cutting it. Even if you don't often sew or at all. The Cricut might make fabric projects fun to try. The rotary blade cuts through fabric with ease and makes fabric projects tempting to try. Who hasn't thought of making a quilt? The Cricut even has quilt kits that are precut and help to make your first quilt pretty easy. More about fabric in the sewing chapter.

There are hundreds of sewing and crafting projects just waiting for you to try. The rotary blade changes everything and the ability to mark and cut patterns literally "cuts" time down when it comes to sewing.

Iron on

Remember the old iron-on projects and patterns you used to buy at craft stores and how the patterns were limited to just what you saw hanging on display? With the Cricut, the patterns are endless for any pattern you can imagine and the projects are endless as well. Along with the patterns, the different materials offer as many possibilities as you can imagine as well, with a matte, glossy and metallic. And then there are patterned prints and holographic prints that offer shimmer and shine. A SportsFlex material for iron-on helps the user have a flexible material the moves with even with the most active of sports enthusiasts.

Paper

Originally, it was thought the best use of the Cricut maker was for cutting paper and making scrapbooks. There are still many users who do just that. And the Cricut is growing and still making more and more patterns as scrapbookers keep growing as well. It is very common at scrapbooking retreats to see almost every person there to haul out their personal Cricut maker as they begin their fun each day! Paper offers a variety of projects in both the simplest forms and more advanced forms. Now the Cricut maker has evolved from just cutting paper to also cutting foil, cardstock and poster board, to name a few for the happy scrapbooker or card maker.

Heavier Material

There are several tools in the Cricut Maker. One is the knife blade. The knife blade is used to cut a variety of materials. The knife blade is made to cut heavier materials such as leather, faux leather and types of light wood. Balsa wood, basswood, Cricut chipboard, craft foam, and matboard to name a few. When cutting the heavier materials, make sure to use the correct mat that will hold the heavier material, so the material does not slip during the cutting process.

The Cricut Maker and Your Computer

The first thing to do when you are ready to get started using your Cricut Maker is to plug it in and turn it on. Your Cricut Make has a USB cord to plug into your computer. Plug it in and go to the design, Cricut setup button on your browser. Follow the instructions and when you get to the step that indicates you are ready for your first project, then your Cricut Maker is ready as well!

This process is fairly easy and updates should happen automatically when your Cricut is hooked up to your computer.

Chapter 3

Beginner Projects to Make

Now that we know what materials to use with the Cricut Maker and a basic understanding of how the Cricut maker works, it is time to start making some simple projects with the new machine. There are 50 beginning projects you receive when you get your new Cricut Maker. There are also projects that are labeled "Make it Now." These are projects any beginner can complete. Again, the key is getting all your materials ready before starting your project

.

Paper Crafts

Paper crafts are among the easiest to start with your new Cricut Maker. Use card stock of 60lb or 110lb purchased from a local craft store or paper supply store and begin! If you begin with paper crafts, you are not wasting expensive materials.

Paper Flowers

Try making paper flower corsages. There is a bit of a learning curve when it comes to making paper flowers, but once you get the hang of it, you will never buy another silk or artificial flower again. Choose various colors and paper textures and experiment with this.

Paper Greeting Cards

Many people buy their first Cricut Maker with the idea of making greeting cards. If you look on Etsy, you will see dozens of people selling home-made cards and earning extra money using their Cricut Maker to make these cards. Many users recommend a **Cricut Access Membership.** This will give you access to thousands of images, hundreds of fonts and discounts off purchases for supplies and accessories.

Paper Home Décor

Brighten any season of the year when decorating your home and using your Cricut machine to make various seasonal decorations to accent your home. The possibilities are endless.

Foam Projects

Your Cricut even cuts foam! DIY foam stamps are one of the easiest beginner's projects to complete. You will be amazed at the dozens and dozens of foam projects you can create using your Cricut Maker!

Personalized Mugs, Plates, Jars, and More

Using vinyl to create your own personalized labels for any surface is a snap with this machine. Using SVG files make the projects easy to personalize anything from bags and shirts to your luggage. And don't forget the dishes. Many a penny has been made from personalizing dishes!

Personalized Soap Bottles

Just add clear transfer tape after putting on your own vinyl to make the label waterproof. The personalized soap bottles add a special treat to any bathroom. You can buy blank bathroom supplies at the dollar store and then personalize them for pennies. Or you can buy personalized bathroom supplies for about $15 to $20 each at department stores.

Your Cricut Maker will literally pay for itself by the projects you make for your home alone, not to mention the gifts you make for others.

Welcome Door Mat

Buy a blank doormat and make it your own using SVG files and materials from your Cricut. This can be done for the price of a blank doormat that can be purchased at your local Home Depot or Lowes. So much less expensive than a doormat someone else customizes.

Koozies (An insulator made of foam, neoprene or another fabric that surrounds a container to keep drinks cold)

Koozies can be personalized for weddings and special events. One Cricut user went into business, designing only koozies for weddings and other parties. This is now her full-time job.

Farmhouse Signs

Take a scrap of wood, paint the wood and then use a decal from your Cricut Maker. You have a rustic looking sign that before you paid someone else to make. This is a very simple project. Farmhouse signs are all the rage and the trend just seem to be rising! Customize your own favorite quote and truly make your home designed for your family.

Fabric Imaged Pillows, Blankets, and Furniture

You can put designs from your Cricut Maker on decorative pillows to suit any season. You can also use fabric paint on pillows. Become the decorator you have always wanted to be for a fraction of the cost.

Felt Projects

Anything you can imagine with felt, you can create with your Cricut Maker. Any season and calendar can be enhanced with fun felt projects all created using the Cricut Maker. The Cricut Maker helps people to look forward to every season and every holiday. You can ring in the festivities for your entire family!

Apparel

You can design T-shirts, socks, and shoes. Iron-on or fabric paint. Can you imagine designer shoes for every occasion? Go Chiefs! Or Rams! Or whoever! Everyone loves a team shirt. Think of all the local schools in your area. Go in and offer to make their shirts for a reasonable price once they have a design.

Drawing and Writing with the Cricut

As mentioned in the accessories section of this guide, the Cricut is often used for writing and designing letters, signs, and envelopes. Drawing with the Cricut Maker adds so much to your designs and makes things more personal. Remember, any design can be turned into a drawing with the drawing feature.

Wall Art

You can create amazing different kinds of wall art with the Cricut knife blade combined with Design Space. You can use a pre-made design or your own creation to cut materials made from chipboard, balsa, matboard, poster board, paper, and others. This is perfect for crafting during any holiday season.

Stencils

In the past, you had to buy a premade stencil for every size and pattern you needed, but with a Cricut Maker, you can make stencils on almost any surface using patterns within the available fonts. The stencils and projects you can make are only limited to your imagination.

Leatherwork

The finer blades on the Cricut make it possible to even do craft projects on leather. From earrings to hair clips to small bags, leatherwork and faux leatherwork are all the rage.

Chapter 4

Advanced Projects

When people start getting used to their Cricut Maker and making more projects with their machine, often users comment that they like purchasing the Cricut Access for $9.99 a month, especially if using the Cricut becomes more than just a hobby. Cricut Access has a library of over 30,000 non-licensed images, 1000 projects, and 400 fonts. If you pay by the year, this product figures out to be $7.99 per month. There are more savings available through this service and Cricut Access can help you with more advanced projects.

3D Flower Bouquets

To make 3D flowers using your Cricut Maker start by buying different colored scrapbook paper of the colored flowers you want in your bouquets. You can find the patterns for 3D flowers in the Cricut Design Space application. You also need a glue gun, hole punch and greenwood sticks for the flowers, floral foam, and floral tape. You will need to get those items from a crafting store.

Once you find the patterns you want to use in your Cricut Design Space, choose the sizes and then cut the flowers in a variety of different shapes. After the design has been cut, the weed away the paper you are not using. The flower will be left in a circular shape. This is when you punch a hole in the center of the innermost part of the shape. Put one of your green sticks through the hole and then use the florist wire to help wrap over the circular part of the bottom of the flower and wind the flower around the stick.

Starting from the outside of the circle then roll the flower into the center until it finally forms a nice flower. You will have to pinch it as you roll the paper together. When you get to the end, use the glue to stick the last end and press the flower down onto its circular base to stay. Wrap the stem in florist tape. When you have several flowers, you can arrange in a bouquet using florist foam. There are some brides who are using these bouquets at weddings because they are so beautiful and cost-effective.

Formal Place Cards

Thanksgiving is a fun time to set a formal table complete with place cards. Your family will appreciate the special thought you put into decorating and putting their names on place cards to complete your Thanksgiving table setting. If your family is like so many, you may have people who need gluten-free, or who might be vegan, vegetarian. You can make labels for different dishes along with name badges.

First, you must think of your color scheme and then get the pens to go with this scheme. There are so many beautiful Fall colors to make a Thanksgiving-themed named place card. Make sure you have white cardstock to make the name card.

On your Cricut, start by making two rectangles. The first should be 3.5" by 2" and the other one was 3.25" by 1.75". Change the smaller rectangle to a writing rectangle by clicking the image and change the icon from the scissors icon to the pen icon.

Finally, add the image. The "Yours Truly" font is almost like cursive if you change the letter spacing to -0.76 so the letters will connect without spacing. This will look like cursive once you get the spacing correct. Double-check to make sure you have it set as a writing font and set in the same color as your written rectangle. Choose the color you feel looks the best in your color scheme.

Once you experiment and practice, these place cards will literally take you 5 minutes to print and cut and your Thanksgiving table will have a touch of elegance your family deserves.

Personalized Christmas Baubles

These Christmas ornaments are inspired by Rae Dunn. Now if you don't know who or what Rae Dunn is, you are not alone. However, Rae Dunn is a beautiful line of dishes that are simple and fun. If you look up the name, you will go, "Oh, yes. I know this." These ornaments are inspired by this line of dishes. Most of her dishes are white with tall black letters.

The first thing you need to do to make these ornaments is to pick your surface. You can use clear Christmas balls, or colored white balls, another color of balls, or even flat round disks that hang on trees. You can find these at any craft or hobby store. Make a list of fun Christmas words. The fun font to use for this is called the Skinny. Now if you are planning to sell these you have to use the font on Creative Market called Wanderlust. This font has a commercial license. You must choose the size of font based on the size of your ornament, but probably no bigger than 1.5 inches tall.

After you cut each word out then you have to weed in between each letter. This does take some time because the letters are detailed. Apply transfer tape on top of the phrases and rub these down really well. Cut them apart and then it's time to apply to the ornaments. The trick is to apply the vinyl at a 45-degree angle and unfold a corner, so the transfer tape goes on smoothly. It might take some practice, but once the letters are all down you can peel off the tape and you have new ornaments or lovely gifts!

Cake Toppers

Never before has decorating wedding cakes or any cakes for that matter, been so easy. To make a cake topper displaying the word *love* in gold glitter you need the following materials: the Cricut weeding tool and spatula, 2 bamboo skewers, Mod Podge or Superglue, glitter cardstock, preferably 2-sided and a paintbrush

The first step is to load the image of the word "love" that you want to print out with your Cricut Maker. It should be kind of elaborate. Once you get the image you want, save and tag it. Size the image to the width of the top of your cake. Center the image on the cutting mat. Select the glitter cardstock in Cricut Design Space. Weed out the cake topper and use the scraper to easily remove from the cutting mat.

Glue the cake topper on the bamboo skewers. And your cake topper is complete. You can add colors and varieties for any occasion. This does not have to be for a wedding. You can get fancy with birthdays, anniversaries, promotions, and retirement parties as well.

T-Shirt Printing

Many people actually get the Cricut Make to design and print T-shirts. The easiest way to design and make your own T-shirts is with vinyl. To make a T-shirt, you will upload an SVG file with the lettering and the graphic of your choice or you can design one of your own. You can use any T-shirt of your own choosing. You will also use a fine point blade for the cutting of the design. The light grip map will be used and a regular iron. One sheet of parchment paper is also useful.

Once you save your files on your computer, click on the upload option located on the left panel of the canvas area. When you see the screenshot below, then you can upload an image or a pattern. Click on that and select the SVG file from your computer. The first time is the hardest. Once you do this a few times, it is like riding a bike. You will find it gets much easier and faster. Once you click on the image, it will become a recently loaded image, so then it is easy to find.

When you click insert images, the file then shows up in your Design Space Canvas area. Basically, after that, you resize to fit the image to the T-shirt and Voila!, you are ready. Once you resize, you have to attach all of the elements. You will have to select all of the layers and attach. The attach button is located at the bottom of the Layers panel. You should see all the words in your canvas area.

The fun thing to do is to use a T-shirt template and line up the design with a template and then you can see how your design will look on the T-shirt. On the left side of the canvas area, there is an icon called templates. When you click on templates, you will be able to look at all of the surfaces available for you to see your different designs.

Once you are happy with how your design looks, click "make it." You will be prompted to connect your machine and follow the cutting process. For vinyl, you have to turn on the mirror option too. You have to do this because you are cutting upside down.

After the vinyl comes out of the machine, place it on the shiny mat side down. Put in the fine point blade and load the mat into the Cricut to cut the vinyl. Once you tap it into the machine, click "make it," and you can sit back and the Cricut do the work! The program will let you know when the design is 100% cut.

When the design is cut, you will weed the excess vinyl away. Be careful that you don't remove important parts. After the weeding, it is time to transfer the vinyl to the shirt. This is why the vinyl was mirrored. Now you are putting the vinyl face down and then you are ironing on over parchment. Do not get your iron too hot. Once the vinyl is down evenly and you are sure all the vinyl is down. Then you can peel the extra transfer tape away. You have a nice T-shirt you have made yourself.

Umbrellas

Umbrellas are going to get wet so to save you the work and the pain of do-overs, buy permanent adhesive vinyl. You will use transfer tape, as usual, to stick the vinyl to the umbrella and the trick is getting the vinyl laid down correctly and pressed pretty firmly.

The nice thing about this project is you can cut small shapes out of vinyl scraps for an umbrella and make something totally unique. Or you can choose SVG files through Design Space. Then go through the same process that you went through to make the umbrellas that are outlined above in the T-shirt process.

There are so many cute things you can put on an umbrella from hearts to flowers, different shapes, multi-colored raindrops and rainbows. These umbrellas can be as colorful and unique as your imagination allows!

Car and Motorbike Stickers

Custom stickers for cars and motorbikes are fun to have and even more fun to design and make for yourself. To use your Cricut Maker to make one or a hundred car stickers just follow these steps:

1. Measure the area where you are putting the sticker.
2. Select your design from a file or make your design on your own. You can combine Cricut, photoshop, etc. and then convert your design into a PGN file and export it into Cricut Design.
3. You will then export the design and enter those dimensions you actually need.
4. Put the vinyl on the sticky mat and then slide it into the Cricut Machine.
5. When it is finished with the Cricut magic, weed the design, put the transfer tape onto the design and make sure you press it down very well. There should be no air bubbles.
6. Clean the surface of where the sticker is going really well if you haven't already.
7. Peel the transfer tape away from the vinyl.
8. Apply the vinyl sticker to your car or motorbike. And you have a professional sticker for your wheels.

You could even make smaller stickers for a child's bike. This would be a fun activity for you and your kids to design together. Let them pour over the different designs and files, then follow the same process and create their stickers as well. Your kids will enjoy being a part of the Cricut Maker process.

Clothes Hangers

If you want to personalize your wedding, for instance, this would be an accessory you might not think about but would be one of the small fun details that help make things special. You could put vinyl names on all of your bridal party hangers for their clothes. How neat would that be!

To make personalized hangers you need, wooden hangers, white vinyl, your scraper tool, weeding tool, transfer tape and of course, your Cricut Maker. You can choose from your set of fonts.

The first step is to measure the top of the hanger area where you are going to put the names. Probably if you bought an average wooden hanger your biggest name will be up to 4 inches wide and 1.5 inches tall.

You will create your names in your Cricut Maker file and be able to choose from the many fonts available. Once you write all of the names you will export the files as an SVG file. Open Design Space and create a new project. Now upload one of the files you just exported. Choose the type of image it is and click continue.

Save the image as a cut image. After it is saved, it is ready to import to your project. You will then see it on your grid. Resize it to fit the dimensions to fit in the middle of what would be your hanger. You might find a template to line up that looks like a hanger.

When you have this lined up just right, place the vinyl on the mat so it sticks, turn the Cricut Maker on and connect to your computer. Set the mat so it will feed into your Cricut machine and click "Go".

Then you will use your weeding tool to cut away excess vinyl. Time for your transfer tape! Cut a piece about the size of your name and take off the backing and place it on the vinyl. Use your scraper tool to press it down to make sure the transfer tape is on it super well. This is important.

Now, you can carefully pull off the white backing from the vinyl, so the vinyl stays attached to the transfer tape. Center it to the middle of your hanger and apply! Use the scraper tool again to make sure the vinyl is attached completely to the hanger. Now, very carefully pull the transfer tape from the vinyl and the hanger. Do this slowly so the vinyl stays in place. And you have one hanger done!

Water Bottles

The nice thing about designing your own projects is you can literally create anything you want. From glitter to shiny. Once you get into using your Cricut, you will notice the design and creating process will take longer than the cutting or the application process.

The water bottle design is created much like the T-shirt design and personalized hangers. If you are using names, you can use cursive, block-printing, and any kind of texture and colors for vinyl. The water bottles make great gifts for literally everyone no matter the age!

One of the fun things about going back to school or going to practice is having a new water bottle. Now all of your kids can have their own personalized water bottles. Make sure you are doing age appropriate. The older cool guys are going to want to keep it simple. Maybe their whole team needs one? Everyone needs a personalized water bottle.

Lampshades

Even lampshades? Yes, even lampshades! Any home decorating you would like to do, Cricut Iron-on makes this possible. Lamps are particularly fun because you can buy a lamp at a garage sale for $2 or $3. And, these lamps are usually in pretty good shape!

Iron-on vinyl has two parts: the liner and then the iron-on vinyl that will be actually ironed onto your project. The liner is used to protect your vinyl during the ironing process. Remember to mirror the image so when it cuts in the Cricut Maker, the image is backwards. This is important because when the image is ironed onto the lamp it will be the correct way facing out.

Remember, you can use your own iron or the Cricut ironing device. If you use your iron, set the iron at cotton/linen with the steam function off. Preheat the iron just a little bit. It will help get the iron setting correctly. Place the image, liner side up. Lay a wet cloth over the design. Apply medium pressure over the iron for 25 or 30 seconds. Or use your Cricut press on medium setting without a wet cloth. You should also apply pressure to the back of the lampshade if you can get to it for good measure. Peel off the liner after it cools and you are finished in a little less than an hour.

Backpacks

Just like umbrellas, cups, and water bottles, people love to personalize their backpacks. Especially the tween crowd loves their golden lettering and their little personalized names and whistles and gadgets. Seriously, kids love to have the little touches on their backpacks that help them feel just a little bit special and identified.

Today, many kids in elementary school go to schools where they wear uniforms. Backpacks and tennis shoes are areas where they can express some sense of style and fashion. And those kids' parents are keeping Cricut users busy all summer with backpack orders!

With Design Space you can even use patterns and registered trademarks from Disney. Here's how you can do just that.

In the Cricut Design Space open the file you'd like. Younger kids love unicorns and Mickey Mouse, so let's start with those as examples. Insert one of those files you want onto the canvas. For the Mickey Mouse, you can create a silhouette to cut out with your Cricut Maker. You can hide certain layers, then change the contours of the others. Or you could use the full-on colorful Mickey Mouse.

To create the unicorn backpack, size the unicorns to 1.5" high. Then spaced them 2" apart and stagger them in rows. This is very easy to do in Design Space. You can use the "align" feature and "distribute" feature to make sure that the grid spaces them out perfect.

If you want to embellish the top of the backpack it will measure about 9" wide by 7" tall. Cut out an 11" x 11" "grid" because you will most likely use 12" x 12" piece of vinyl. For the Mickey Mouse image, size it just under 7" from bottom of the hands to top of the ears so it would fit under the zipper. This pattern cuts off part of the hands to center his face on the backpack front.

Then you can cut the image as you normally would. Make sure you click "Attach" to get all the elements cut like the layout you see on your computer screen. Then you will click "mirror" and cut. Then you will cut the iron on to size and iron the vinyl down onto the backpack. After it is cooled, pull off the plastic backing sheet.

Henna Tattoos

Your Cricut can even design and cut patterns for Henna Tattoos. But first, what is a Henna Tattoo? A Henna tattoo is not permanent and a needle is not used. They have intricate designs and are considered to be a body art form. A henna tattoo is made from dye from the henna plant. The part of the plant that the henna is used from is made into a powder and is mixed with water or tea. The final product is placed into a small bag and then piped onto the skin in very thin lines.

The henna tattoos make up a very detailed pattern and this is where your Cricut Maker comes into the picture.

If you thought the Cricut maker only worked for cutting materials to go only on to various inanimate objects, think again! The Cricut Maker is able to use what you design to make a henna Tattoo!

In the process of making henna tattoos, a friend discovered using waterslide paper. Waterslide paper works by trapping ink between 2 layers of adhesive sheets of paper. One is double-sided so it will stick to your skin. Waterslide paper is also called silhouette temporary tattoo paper.

The way to create the tattoo is by first printing the solid block of your tattoo onto the waterslide paper. You will use Microsoft Word or a similar program. Then you will use your Cricut maker to cut out your design within the block you just printed. While the Cricut cuts the tattoo, there will be no border, so this will make it look more realistic than other temporary tattoos, but at the same time you have to be careful without a border to guide you.

Make sure to use an inject printer only not a laser printer. The materials include:

1. Waterslide paper
2. Cricut Maker
3. Inkjet printer
4. Water
5. Cloth
6. Blade
7. Ruler
8. Scissors

The first step you will take is to create your henna tattoo In Cricut Design Space. Make sure your design is mirrored so you can place it on your skin correctly. Make sure too your dimensions are such that there is some space from the edge of the tattoo will possibly not all get printed.

The difficult part of this is getting the measurements correctly. Depending on whether you work in inches or cm, Design Space currently only works in inches. Here are some easy conversions. 1 inch = 2.54 cm and 1cm = 0.383in. Waterslide paper = 8.5 in x 11in or 21.59cm x 27.94cm.

Text of the Tattoo

For the text of the tattoo basically use the text function in the Cricut Design Space of your machine to write out what you want your tattoo to say. After that, you will upload your image. This will make the image easier to mirror.

Lines of the Tattoo

This is again pretty basic by inserting the image from Cricut Design Space and size the markings to the correct measurements you want them to be for the tattoo.

Design of the Tattoo

For images, choose any image that you prefer for your tattoo and when you upload it to Cricut Design Space, you can clean up any image background if there is anything you want cost-effective, so just the image shows for your tattoo. It's a very slick way to make a temporary tattoo.

Match all of the dimensions of the tattoo in Design Space because remember, what you see on the screen is what is going to print out! It is possible to choose a different pattern or color. Make sure you print the pattern on the glossy side of the waterslide paper.

Use Design Space to cut the images. After placing the images in Design Space, place the waterslide paper onto the Cricut cutting sheet to make the cuts. Use the vinyl setting. Once the Cricut is finished cutting, they use scissors to rough out each cut, leaving a slight border.

Next use the blade to take away the area of the sticky sheet that covers the tattoo design. For the wording, remove the vinyl that makes up the letters, so you have the same word made out of the vinyl that is taken away, leaving the correct inked area exposed. This will be sticky so be careful. It is critical that this is done carefully as any of the naked ink will stick to your skin.

Place your new henna tattoo on your skin where you want it to go and press it to stick down. Get a moistened washcloth. This should be pretty wet, but not dripping wet. Push the wet cloth on the back of the paper of the tattoo and make sure the entire paper is wet evenly. Leave on for at least 20 seconds. It may begin to slide off and when it does, you can begin to move the rest of the paper off gently

Voila! You now have a new tattoo! It will wash off, so be careful!

Subject Notebooks

Making stylish subject labels is a terrific idea to make each of the school notebooks stand out. You will need:

- Notebooks, the ones with the plastic/poly covers and they work well, Easy to find plain ones with different colors but similar.
- Cricut Maker

- White vinyl shows up best
- Transfer tape

The first thing you will need to do is create your labels. You can set type you want for math, science, etc... and find little icons for each.

To make your own labels, open your Cricut Design Space and type in any keyword you want to use, like "Math" Choose the font you want and then make spacing adjustments so this label looks exactly the way you want it to be cut in the vinyl.

If you want to add images you can find lots of simple line designs in Design Space that will work perfectly for this project. Just type in either the subject "Science" or "Math" to see what comes up and chose an image, For example, to find an image for a test tube for the subject of science you would type in that word and then click on the image and move it over to go with your word. You can center it and arrange the picture to go however you want it to go with your word. Then you can cut the word and image on your vinyl.

Cut the designs out of vinyl and weed the cut designs. Then use transfer tape to place labels on the notebook covers. Easy peasy, but unique and fun for the kids to take to school all ready for each subject!

Faux Leather Earrings

These earrings are as fun to make as they are to wear! And, they make fantastic gifts for any occasion! Faux leather is thinner than actual leather so you can use a regular fine point blade on your Cricut Maker.

Materials:

faux leather and perhaps the foil also for added bling
earring hooks
jump rings
needle nose pliers
leather hole punch
Cricut Maker to cut your leather
A way to iron foil if you use it

First, pick out a design. You can download earring designs from any number of bloggers or look on Design Space. When you cut the faux leather layer, be sure to select "faux leather" as your material and mirror your image. If you use foil for the more bling to your earring, the foil vinyl layer should be set to "foil vinyl iron on" and also mirrored.

If you do decide to cut out the foil vinyl iron-on layer, you'll want to weed the vinyl and then iron the designs onto your earrings before you go any further. You can use the Cricut EasyPress. For faux leather and foil iron-on with the EasyPress mat, the recommended temperature is 255 for 30 seconds. Once you press your iron-on, let it cool before removing the protective liner. Or you can use your regular iron. Use the cotton setting and test it first to make sure that is correct.

Some earrings have precut holes and some do not. This is what your leather punch is for. Punch the hole and then put the jump ring through the hole of your earring. Use your needle nose pliers to open up a jump ring and place the end of the ring through the hole. You have earrings that look very expensive!

Personalized Block Night Lights

To make the personalized Block Night Lights you need the following materials:

Glass block, frosted spray paint, white lights, transfer tape, Cricut maker, adhesive vinyl, enamel spray

How to Make this Light

1) Take your glass block outside and spray the entire block with frosted spray paint. Let it dry before you attempt to do any more to the block.

2) When the block is completely dry, spray two light coats of the enamel spray. Let the block dry in between each coat of enamel.

3) Now you can work on want you want to put on your night light. There are several patterns available in Design Space or you can design your own based on what your children or whoever you are making this for enjoyment. If they are into sports, you can make different sports shapes, like baseball equipment, tennis, or volleyball equipment, etc.

4) Load these designs from your computer into your Cricut Maker for the cuts.

5) After your Cricut Maker has made all the cuts and you have all the cuts in all the colors you have chosen to use then you will do the weeding process and get rid of the excess vinyl.

6) Center your vinyl on the dryer glass block that you painted. Now you are going to use your painter's tape to tape the bottom of the largest piece of words.

7) Gently, lift up your words and pictures if you printed any and peel off the backing paper. Smooth this down and make sure it is secure. Peel off the transfer tape and then press everything down until you know it is secure. Scrape it completely down.

8) Put the white lights inside. Add ribbon or any other decoration you choose, plug in and enjoy!

Jigsaw Puzzle from a Photo

Why buy a bunch of jigsaw puzzles from the store when you can make your own out of your own photos? Plus, you have full control of the number of pieces!

All you need is the following materials: chipboard, 2 pieces of 2 mm, 2 printable vinyl, painter's tape and of course your Cricut maker, a knife blade, and a printer.

Then just follow these 9 steps:

1) Go to Cricut Design Space and search for "puzzle" in the image section. Start with an 8 x 8 puzzle for your first time.
2) Upload a photo of your choice to Design Space and save it as a print.
3) Because you have the jigsaw puzzle section open, you can now line this photo up with the puzzle file on the screen to make sure they are the same size and in line.
4) Trim any edges with the slice function if you feel you need to do that action.
5) Now print the photo on the vinyl.

6) Attach the chipboard to the heaviest grip mat with painter's tape. Cut the first layer using the heavy chipboard setting.

7) Remove the backing off of the vinyl photo and apply it to the other piece of chipboard. Make sure you are leaving a border. This will be important later. Scrape the photo down very well. Make sure there are no bubbles.

8) Now, tape down the chipboard with the photo on the mat and load the mat to cut.

9) Glue the rims of the puzzle together and then insert the pieces that are not glued. This is why the rims were important. So, the two pieces of chipboard could be glued together to make the edge of the puzzle. Now you have a puzzle of your favorite photo!

Glitter Tumblers

Glitter tumblers can make for great giveaways for any occasion.

Here's what you need: stainless steel tumbler, Mod Podge, dry paintbrush for Mod Podge, glitter, dry paintbrush for wiping away glitter spray paint, epoxy resin, painter's tape, rubber gloves, stir sticks, plastic cups, vinyl, Cricut Maker

Once again, you are just 9 steps away to add that glitter touch to a boring stainless-steel tumbler.

1) Thoroughly clean the tumbler.
2) Apply painter's tape to the top and bottom of the tumbler.
3) Spray-paint the tumbler whatever color you want the undercoat to be. This is not necessary because the tumbler is going to be covered in glitter.
4) Brush coat this tumbler with Mod Podge. Make sure you use long strokes with the Mod Podge. There should be no build-up or no gaps.
5) Now, dump the glitter while turning your tumbler around so it is completely covered. Tap the excess glitter off of the tumbler. Remove the tape.
6) Let the tumbler completely dry. This needs to be overnight.
7) Use an old flat dry brush to remove excess glitter. I would also shake the tumbler outside really well.
8) Add epoxy. Tape off the top again. Mix the epoxy thoroughly and apply. This should seal the glitter. You are going to do this step twice. If you want to continue to turn the tumbler there are tumbler turners you can buy or make.
9) After the epoxy dries, you should clean the tumbler off with rubbing alcohol. If you have vinyl decals now is the time to apply them as well. And repeat the epoxy step and the alcohol step. You will have a unique tumbler!

Additional Note:

Make sure when you use sprays or epoxy, you use all chemicals in a well-ventilated area.

Personalized Tiles

These are actual heavy tiles that are personalized for a special occasion. The birth of a baby, graduation, special birthday, etc.

Materials:

Tile – Home Depot or Lowes. The actual heavy tile you use on a kitchen floor
Vinyl – whatever color you prefer
Ribbon or any other decoration you would like
Transfer paper
Blue painter's tape
Ruler
Rubbing alcohol
Cricut Maker

1) The first step is to put the required words so they line up correctly into your design and then place your vinyl into the Cricut Maker to cut. Put it so the wording is able to mirror onto the tile.
2) Once the vinyl has been cut, use the weeding tool to weed in between the letters and around the outsides, so all you have left are your words.

3) Lay the transfer paper on top of the words and use the scraper to press the paper down onto the vinyl words carefully. Make sure the transfer paper is really onto the words.

4) For good measure, clean the tile with rubbing alcohol. It may be dusty from packing.

5) Now the really fun part! Line up the wording where you want it. Tape it down with painter's tape. Now pull the white paper off of the transfer tape. Then with your scraper, smooth the wording over the vinyl one more time.

6) Pull the transfer paper back slowly and press the vinyl down with a finger to make sure it is nice and smooth.

7) Do the same with all vinyl strips and pictures if any. You may use your ruler if you need to make sure things line up correctly before adhering to the tile.

8) The finished product can include a bow and a stand for the tile. Make sure before you give the tile as a gift, the stand is large enough to hold the tile. They are heavy.

Chapter 5

Extra Accessories and What They Do

There are some Cricut Maker users who swear by using very little extra accessories. Still, many other users also subscribe to Cricut Access. There are clubs and local groups that regularly meet in almost every town and region to compare notes on new ideas, accessories, and supplies.

And then there is Pinterest. Pinterest is a wealth of information and friendship when it comes to using the Cricut Maker. There are hundreds of crafters who post their Cricut Maker videos about how to use the basic supplies and also how to use the accessories.

One popular person on Pinterest told our guide writer that there are certain accessories to for sure get once a person is often crafting with their Cricut Maker. She gave us a pretty complete list and why to include this list.

Essential Tool Kit

First, the "Essential Tool Kit," is the accessory she believes every Cricut user should own. Well, if you use your Cricut often and like to make a lot of projects, this accessory is the most complete kit and biggest bang for your money. This kit contains:

> ➢ Tweezers for grabbing thin materials, small pieces, and holding them. This tool also helps people with unsteady hands.
> ➢ Scissors with a protective blade cover.
> ➢ A replacement blade for the trimmer that is with your Cricut Maker
> ➢ A paper trimmer for materials up to 12 inches wide
> ➢ A scoring blade for the trimmer

> ➢ Weeder to remover tiny scraps
> ➢ A spatula to lift cut pieces up from your working mats. Like lifting up cookies off of a baking sheet.
> ➢ A scraper for scraping material scraps off your cutting mats.
> ➢ A scoring stylus. You use this to add fold lines to paper projects.

Depending on where you purchased this Essential Tool Kit, prices may range from $16.00 to $35.00.

Cricut Pens

Cricut Pens are another must-have and those can be purchased as an accessory or as a set from a local craft store.

Our Cricut friend suggested just to go ahead and buy the Cricut Ultimate Fine Point Set. This is often on sale for less than the retail price of $34.99. Currently, the price is $24.49 for this set at the time of writing this guide. However, as stated previously, many markers will fit in the Cricut Maker. You just have to experiment with colors and brands to see which markers you prefer.

Scoring Wheel

Another nice to have accessory is the **scoring wheel** if you do a lot of papercrafts. The Essential Tool Kit does come with a scoring stylist, but the scoring wheel is so nice for crafting with paper. You get better and cleaner lines with a scoring wheel.

Brayer and Broad Piece Tweezer Set

One last piece of advice for extra accessories is to buy the **brayer and broad piece tweezer set.** The brayer is used to clamp down the fabric to your mat. The broader tweezers make it even easier than the other tweezers to pick up cut fabric pieces. This also helps to keep oil from the mats. You may think your hands are clean and they are, but your fingers still have natural oil on them and this shortens the life of the adhesive on the mats.

Sewing Kit

Some people also recommend the sewing kit. The sewing kit is probably a goal for a person who does a lot of quilting and other sewing projects. This would be a nice purchase and probably save hours and steps in the long run with these extra tools. In the kit you will find thread snips, measuring tape, a leather thimble, pins and cushion, fabric shears that will even cut leather and multiple layers of fabric and a seam ripper. The sewing kit is highly recommended. Many people might have these items, but it's just nice to have all these items together in one place.

Bonded-Fabric Blade + Housing. This is a drag blade made from German carbide steel. If you need to cut bonded, fusible, basted, or stabilized fabric, this blade is an accessory you can buy.

Washable Fabric Pen – This pen is used for drawing on fabric. This draws patterns and any drawings you choose as well — a very good accessory to have and highly recommended.

The Cricut Easy Press

The Cricut Easy Press seems to be another accessory most Cricut users usually buy. You can always use a household iron to apply vinyl iron-on transfers or other transfers, but people who get the Cricut Easy Press seem to never look back to their household iron when making projects. This Cricut Easy Press usually starts at around $140 and goes up from there depending on the size.

Crafters who use their iron advise to at least buy a middle of the road iron. The advantages of using a household iron are that a household iron is easy to store, it's lightweight, it's easier to maneuver over surfaces that are not perfectly flat like tennis shoes. And, the household iron is a more frugal purchase.

The disadvantages of a household iron are that the exact temperature is hard to regulate and if the temps get suddenly too hot, your project can be ruined in seconds. Sometimes when using a regular iron your project can also bubble in spots. Also, the project sometimes doesn't press well. You have to repress. Foil does not do well with an iron at all.

With the Cricut Easy Press, the temperature can be set for a certain degree and regulated. The Easy Press was made to press vinyl, so vinyl adheres perfectly. The heat distribution is even throughout the whole press. It heats up in 1 minute.

The Easy Press comes in several sizes. The Cricut Easy Press comes in different colors and pleasing to the eye.

Sticky Mats

The sticky mats add confusion to using the Cricut Maker. Sometimes it's hard to figure out which mat to use for which project. Certain mats are less or more sticky than other mats. The trick is to figure out which one is to be used for the project you are working on at the time.

Having the right degree of stickiness is actually doing to determine the success of the end product of your project. It almost sounds silly, but it's so true. If a sticky mat isn't sticky for instance, this will cause sliding around and may cause miscuts in your vinyl or whatever material you are cutting.

The **green** mat will come in your box with your Cricut Maker. This will help with most of your crafting projects. This will hold down vinyl, card stock, paper, etc.. If you have a use for lighter weight material like tissue or vellum, you should purchase a **blue** light grip mat. For heavier materials such as tagboard or leather and similar heavy materials, a **purple** sticky mat should be bought and used. Finally, the **pink** mat is for fabric. When using the mats, use this guide as a rule of thumb for choosing mats based on material thickness, texture and makeup.

Cricut Mystery Box

A lot of crafters don't know about the Cricut Mystery Box, but this is available from time to time on the Cricut website for a price of between $29 to $39. And people receive anywhere from $80 to $120 worth of supplies in this box. One crafter said she received extra blades, a mat, instructions for unique crafts, vinyl, cardstock, and other materials worth up to $100. This is something that isn't available often and is totally unnecessary. It's just if you want to spend the money to see what you might get.

Cricut Free Cut Friday

Every week on each Friday, Cricut will release some cut files for free. You can only use those files in that next week. You access those files through Design Space.

Oracal Vinyl and Siser EasyWeed Heat Transfer - Starter Sample Pack

The Starter Sample Pack is a sample pack containing 64 sheets of different colors of vinyl. Each piece is 12 x 12 and the pack is enough for several crafting projects. If you like lots of color pop, this sample pack is for you. Now some people prefer to use the basic black and white, so maybe purchasing the sample pack might be a waste of money. The cost of this pack is roughly $34.00. These packs also make great gifts for friends who might have a Cricut Maker.

Washable Fabric Pen

Often clothing or fabric patterns are confusing. The washable fabric pen is able to be placed in the Cricut Maker in the A slot. So many of the patterns included in Cricut Access have the options to have the patterns marked and numbered by the pen. They also have the seam allowance drawn on the material by the pen. This makes the sewing so much easier when you get to that part of the project. This pen is a bargain at $2.99.

Cricut Bonded Fabric Blade

The Rotary blade is great for sewing. However, if you are cutting bonded, basted, or fusible fabric, it is a good idea to get the Bonded Fabric Blade. The Bonded Fabric Blade is a pretty heavy-duty blade set to cut those mentioned fabrics easier than the rotary blade that comes with your Cricut Maker. The price of this Blade is $34.99.

Cricut Maker Engraving Tip

This Engraving Tip is $24.99 but is worth the price if you plan to engrave several objects or have an engraving business. It is very easy to install into your quick snap housing unit.

Cricut BrightPad (Formerly known as Lightbox)

The Cricut Bright Pad is the **brilliant** crafting partner that helps to light up projects for easier crafting and reducing eye strain. Use it for weeding, quilting, tracing and more. It's very light, durable and thin for comfort and ease of portability. With its very low profile, you can trace sitting at a table or watching your favorite program on the couch. The bright pad sells for between $45 and $55 at various locations.

Chapter 6

Sewing and Engraving with Your Cricut Maker

Sewing and engraving with your Cricut Maker need a separate chapter because the Cricut Maker has just blown up the sewing world. There are thousands of sewing projects you can make with your Cricut Maker. If you have not done much sewing, the Cricut Maker makes sewing so much easier, and if you do a lot of sewing, the Cricut Maker will save you time and effort.

Engraving is located in this chapter as well because it is such a specialty craft. But first, let's talk about sewing and the new features with your Cricut Maker.

Sewing with Your Cricut Maker

Unlike the Cricut explorer, there are so many more options in Cricut Design Space that make sewing a delight. You might be saying, "I don't need a machine to tell me what I already know about sewing." But the Cricut Maker offers so much more.

Because the Cricut Maker comes with a **rotary blade**, sewing becomes so much easier. Because of this rotary blade, you are able to load up the Cricut maker with your material and the machine will make your cuts for you without a hitch. They are smooth and clean and in a small fraction of the time it would have taken you to make the cuts by hand.

Cricut Maker also has a Bonded-Fabric Blade + Housing. This is a drag blade made from German carbide steel. If you need to cut bonded, basted, fusible, or stabilized fabric, this blade is an accessory you can buy. There is also a fabric pen for writing on fabric. And the Cricut Maker does have the technology to draw on your fabric. This will also draw your pattern lines out before they are cut. Let us repeat. The Cricut Maker marks the patterns and then cuts the patterns for you!

Now you can design and cut a project that uses fabric and iron on quickly and easily in the same program. The design studio has some very cute stuffed animal projects that use iron-on as the face on a fabric stuffed toy. There is also an adorable globe that is made from fabric and the countries are made from iron-on. The iron on has a seam allowance built right into it so you can add the iron on and then sew the project. So fun!

A New Sewing Partner – Simplicity

The pattern designer and developer, Simplicity has partnered up with Cricut and has offered over 200 patterns currently. More are coming. Currently, there are patterns for luggage tags, puppets, small backpacks, purses, small bags with zippers, fabric coasters, and so much more. Simplicity is the premier name in sewing. When we think of sewing and patterns we think of Simplicity. And now, we are going to think of the Cricut Maker.

Riley Blake Designs

Cricut has also partnered with Riley Blake Designs to make quilts and offer some beautiful fabric lines. You can find these in Cricut Access. These gorgeous fabrics come in squares cut to match your mats, so all you have to do is design the cuts you will make out of those squares before you sew your quilt pieces together.

A bonus is offered when you buy a Cricut Maker. You will automatically receive 50 free project files which include two quilt patterns and quite a few sewing patterns as well. The other nice free inclusion is a material list you are able to view on your phone, tablet, or laptop so you will know what to buy from the sewing or craft store when you go. Part of the confusion when sewing is figuring out exactly how much to buy of trim, etc. The instructions included with your Cricut Maker eliminates this confusion.

If you have never quilted before, now is the time to jump in and try. Get into the file and find out what you need. Follow the prompts and before you know it, you will be sewing your squares together. Riley Blake Designs has such beautiful fabrics, you cannot go wrong with those or you can purchase your own at your local fabric store. Now is the time to try this if you haven't made a quilt before. You can start with a simple pattern and grow from there.

Some of the free project patterns included with the purchase of your new Cricut Maker include, embroidered glasses case, little zipper bow pouch, quilted tablet holder, star quilt pillow, Christmas stockings, tabletop tool caddie, table runner, and more. Can you imagine everyone in your family having matching Christmas stockings you have made with your new Cricut Maker? As stated above, the pattern is included with your new Cricut Maker.

You can access over 500 Simplicity patterns with the new plan in place for Cricut users. When you buy a pattern, you will have lifetime access to it through your Cricut Access Subscription. Remember this is a subscription for 9.99 per month and gives you free access to thousands of free projects and free patterns as well as some you may pay for. The ones you do pay for, you have access to all the sizes for example if the item is in clothing.

Step by Step Instructions

This is a dream come true for visual learners! Cricut Maker is providing step by step instructions and photos with every step so you as the sewer know exactly what to do with each step in every single craft and sewing project. They also give you the material list and everything down to the very last assembly instruction.

The instructions also tell you the difficulty of the project and how long it should take from start to finish. When you are ready to use your Cricut on these projects you can also use your Snap Mat function. You can lay the fabric you are using on the mat that is best for fabric. Then use the Snap Mat function to take a photo of the mat. Because of this, you will be able to see a photo of your fabric and mat in Design Space and can then position your cuts exactly where you want them. This will work great when you are using fabric scraps for quilting or other crafts.

Most people who sew, have tons of left-over fabric and sometimes that is nice. However, often this leftover fabric just becomes a big dust trap. When sewing using a Cricut Maker there is so much less waste. The cuts are more precise and can be lined up closer together. Another bonus is because Cricut Maker instructions will tell you exactly what to buy, you will have fewer overages in the beginning.

Engraving with Your Cricut Maker

The Cricut Maker is able to engrave plastics, acrylics, metal clay, and flat metal (copper, bronze, silver, and other soft metals such as aluminum. The engraved foil wrapping paper is really pretty.

When engraving, place the material down on the mat that holds thicker material. Tape the material down for extra security, but not over the area you are going to engrave. Switch out your tool to the engraving tip. Use the preview screen in Design Space and then move the design you are using to the corresponding position.

If your material is extra thick, make sure you put the white star wheels on the roller bar all the way to the right. This makes sure the thicker material is able to clear the area and does not streak up or have track marks. You also have to make sure your material is not wider than 11 inches. If your material is pretty stiff you might have to help guide the material through the machine or at least support the machine mat.

Be careful when the engraving is finished. The left-over fragments of metal might be sharp. Brush them away before handling the project you have engraved.

Sewing Projects:

Sewing a Banner

❖ Cricut Maker
❖ Iron-on Vinyl Whatever color you want.
❖ 12×24-inch piece of canvas or duck cloth
❖ 12 x 12 cutting Fabric adhesive mat
❖ Regular grip cutting mat
❖ Sewing Machine
❖ Thread in coordinating colors
❖ Fabric Scissors, pins, and pincushion (You'll love the sewing kit from Cricut that has all the tools you need to start sewing)
❖ Iron or Cricut Easy Press
❖ Yarn or twine
❖ A dowel that is 12" long or longer
❖ Optional Cricut Bright Pad for weeding

1) Open your banner of choice in Design Space. Using your Cricut, cut your banner, heart and words.
2) Weed the vinyl leaving cut pieces behind.
3) Fold your canvas in half so that the two tips of the banner are lined up. Measure down 1.5 inches from your folded edge on each side and mark with a straight pin. Pin or wonder clip the rest of your banner in place. Using a 1/4-inch seam allowance, sew from the straight pin on the right that you used to measure 1.5 inches

down, down around and back up to the second straight pin that you used to measure 1.5 inches down.

4) Using one of the gaps where you didn't sew, flip your banner right side out. Push out your corners and edges and press into place.

5) Slip your dowel into the top of your banner. Place a straight pin on one side slightly below where the dowel is so there is enough room for the dowel to slide in and out of the banner. Measure how far down your pin is and measure and pin the same distance on the opposite side. Remove your dowel and it's time for the last sewing step! To give your banner a finished look, stitch along each of the edges of the banner using a 1/8-inch seam allowance and then across the top of the banner using your pins as a guide for where to stitch.

6) Using the instructions on your iron-on packaging or your Easy Press, press your heart onto your banner. Then place your words onto the banner.

7) If your dowel is too long, trim your dowel to the desired length. You can use sandpaper to smooth out the ends. Tie yarn to the ends of the dowel. You are done. This actually takes between 20 and 30 minutes.

Creating a Mini Kleenex Holder

Materials:

Cricut Maker
Sewing Machine
Adhesive cutting mat
Travel-sized Kleenex
Iron
Enough material to cut 5- 4.5 inch by 6.5-inch rectangles
Matching thread

1) Open the Kleenex Holder file in Cricut Design. When you are making the Kleenex holder to keep it simple, you should cut all of your pieces from one fold of fabric. At least for your first Kleenex holder. Then the next time, you can use multiple pieces of fabric and change the color of every rectangle piece. You can try that your first time. It's up to you! There will be four pieces that you will be using for the top of the holder cutting from one piece of fabric and a final piece used for the bottom from a different piece of fabric. This will go on a different mat.

2) You will click "Make it" and have the Cricut make cut your fabric after you have everything completely laid out and have the design loaded up in Cricut Design.

3) Fold and iron two of the pieces of fabric the long way with the print facing out. Then you will also fold and iron

two of the other pieces of fabric widest way also with the print facing out. The fifth piece will remain flat.

4) Place the piece of fabric that you are using for the bottom of your project flat on the table. This is also with the print side facing up. Now you will also lay out the 4 top pieces of the fabric. With each piece you also want to keep the ragged edge turned so it is lined up with the raw edge of the bottom piece of fabric. These will need to be lined out almost the way you would if you were putting a box together that you might use tape instead of sewing.

5) Take the top long piece and the right-side short piece with the top edge overlapping the previous piece you laid down. Now, the bottom long piece with the right sides just going over the sides of the bottom of the prior piece you placed before it. The left piece should overlap the other piece you laid down. The side that is up, will face the inside of your Kleenex holder. Now you are going to turn all the pieces so they are facing the opposite way.

6) Make sure all the edges are lined up and pin into place.

7) Use a straight stitch on all four sides and leave a ½ inch seam allowance.

8) Use a zig-zag stitch around all sides of your Kleenex holder. Line up the inside part of your stitch as close to

your other stitch as possible. Trim away the excess fabric and trim corners.

9) Flip inside out and put your little Kleenex packet inside.

Passport Holder

Do you know someone who is always on the go? Well a personalized passport holder is the perfect gift!

Materials:

- ❖ One 12.5-inch by 6.5-inch piece of fabric for the outside of your passport holder (This fabric will be referred to as print A).
- ❖ One 12.5-inch by 6.5-inch piece of fabric for the lining of your passport holder (This fabric will be referred to as print B).
- ❖ One 12.5-inch by 6.5-inch piece of fusible fleece inside your passport holder to give it a bit of structure.
- ❖ Two 3.25-inch by 4.5-inch of pieces of fabric. This is to use for the outside pocket of your passport. This can be the same print or a different print. The advice is not to make a passport holder super flashy.
- ❖ Sewing Machine
- ❖ Iron
- ❖ Thread in coordinating colors
- ❖ Fabric Scissors, pins and pincushion

1) Cut your fabric with your scissors to 12.5 by 6.5. Your Cricut Maker might make a more exact cut.

2) Once your fabric is cut into pieces, lay the fusible side of the fleece facing up on whatever surface you are going to iron on. Lay the 12.5 by 6.5-inch piece of fabric (this is the fabric you want on the outside of the passport holder), on top of the fusible fleece with the pattern or the colored side you want to see facing up. Aline all the edges and then iron these together following packaging directions of the fleece. This should fuse fairly quickly and easily.

3) Lay the fused piece of material you just ironed on your work surface with the printing side still facing up. Now take the next piece of 12.5 by 6.5-inch of fabric that is for the inside of the passport holder on top of the fused piece with the printed side facing down. Line up all the edges and then pin or wonder clip in place.

4) Using a straight stitch, sew around all 4 edges of the rectangle using a ¼ inch seam allowance. Make sure to leave a one-inch gap between where you start sewing and where you are able to turn your project inside out.

5) When you finish sewing, turn your passport holder inside out so now the passport is right side out. Iron down your edges so the passport holder is laid flat. Don't forget to clip the corners before turning the passport holder inside out.

6) The last pieces of cloth are for the pocket. Lay those pieces on top of each other. Line up the edges with the

printed sides of the fabric facing each other. You will pin those pieces in place.

7) Sew around your pocket so it has a 1/8 inch sewing allowance.

8) Figure out where you want your pocket. The passport holder should be folded in half so the passport lays inside. Fold the edges of the holder to create a small pocket for the edges of your passport. Now, fold those edges over. It should be about two inches on each side. Iron those edges and remove your passport.

9) Open your passport holder back up so that it is one continuous flat rectangle. Sew on the pocket now with a 1/8-inch seam allowance. Sew up and down along the sides to make sure the pocket is secure. Make sure you do the same thing along the bottom.

10) Stretch the passport holder so that it is flat. Sew a 1/8-inch seam allowance along the two shorter edges of your passport holder. Lay your passport holder so fabric A is facing down. Fold the two outside edges back in towards the center using the ironed edge that you pressed before as a guide. Pin or wonder clip into place. Sew around all edges with 1/8-inch seam allowance and you are finished!

Terry Cloth Bibs

Terry Cloth Bibs are the best bibs for a baby who is cutting teeth. Not only is the terry cloth absorbent, but it is a soft material designed to be gentle for the baby's skin. Terry Cloth is originally made from cotton which is a natural fiber. Choose cotton Terry Cloth when making a bib for a little one.

Materials:

Sewing Machine
Walking foot – feeds the terry cloth easier
SVG cut file
Cricut Maker
Pink fabric Mat

Instructions

1) To make a terry cloth bib you need to use the 12 x 14 fabric grip mat. This is the mat that will hold your fabric so it doesn't slide. Terry cloth tends to give off fuzz, so to avoid that, you can press a piece of freezer paper to the back of your material before putting it onto the mat. This should help keep your material down as well.
2) Upload the SVG pattern for baby bibs or any pattern in Simplicity for bibs. It should be able to fit on an 8 x 8 mat. You can make it a little larger possibly for a burp cloth, but do not go smaller.
3) Cut the fabric using the rotary blade.

4) Clip or pin the two pieces of your pattern of the bib together. Place the right sides of the fabric together. This is the softer side. You can feel it to make sure.
5) Start sewing but do not forget your walking foot. The walking foot will really help feed the terry cloth through your sewing machine.
6) You are going to sew around ¾ of the bib. Leave about 3 inches open to turn the bib inside out. Make sure as you turn the bib out, you push out the seams really well.
7) Finish the sewing for the remainder of the bib with a topstitch.

There are literally hundreds of sewing projects you can do with your Cricut Maker. You can get into the patterns and crafts that are available through Design Space, Simplicity, and Pinterest as well as many others that are available. The possibilities are literally endless.

Chapter 7 Social Events

Why Pinterest?

P interest is your new best friend. As a crafter, you probably already know this. You may even have several Pinterest boards and pin often. Pinterest is helpful to you because it has images and links to videos. As a new Cricut Maker user you will be able to ask and answer questions about your Cricut Maker that will ultimately help you to become a better crafter on your machine.

What about joining a Facebook Group?

Facebook now has Interest groups for you to join. These are fun groups of like-minded people who get together because of similar tastes and hobbies. It's like a club and people are saying they are really having fun with their new FB groups. I, indeed, have my own group – come join in the fun!

https://www.facebook.com/groups/1096883060481936/

Parties with Cricut Makers

Friends get together with their Cricut Makers, share ideas and create projects while working together.

Cricut Maker Retreats

Some people do quilting retreats. Now they add their Cricut Maker to the mix. This is a Cricut Maker/Quilting/Crafting Retreat where people actually go to a campground or a designated space for a weekend, to craft, quilt, etc. and enjoy friendship and nature. Someone else is hired to cook, so all the crafter has to do is socialize and craft. Sounds like a dream come true. These retreats happen all over the country!

Craft Fairs

Craft fairs and First Fridays are fun if you don't have to pay very much to set up a booth. Until you are really in business, these are fun events and great ways to meet people. But if there is a large entry fee, we would advise against doing these unless you are seriously going into business. And then, there are better ways for the cost to market your goods. But craft fairs, county fairs and the like are a fun way to meet other crafters and see other projects if there is not a huge cost. Otherwise, give those a pass.

Chapter 8

Are you Ready to Go into Business?

Far too often people who are extremely creative jump into a business before they have actually thought about the business end of the situation. If you are using a Cricut Maker often and people are giving you tons of feedback about your crafts and gifts, it might be a signal that you should go into business with your Cricut Maker. Hundreds of users are doing just that. But what can make you unique and keep you in business for a much longer time?

1. You should have a clear idea of why you want to go into business with your Cricut. Make a list. There may just be one clear reason or there could be 3 or 4, but regardless of how many reasons, define why you want to be in business.

   You might want to be at home with the kids. Have you ever tried to work at home with kids around? Or, perhaps you are making quite a bit with your

Cricut Maker already and have so many orders you cannot keep up on evenings and weekends.

Working outside the home is just not your thing. You have always wanted to be in business for yourself. You enjoy marketing. In fact, you have a marketing degree and you are champing at the bit to be your own boss and use that degree to market your own projects. You think you can take this Cricut business to the top!

Finally, crafting with your Cricut maker feeds your soul. There isn't anything else you would rather do with your life for a job. You can work on projects almost 24/7 and it doesn't bother you. Even when you are not working, you are thinking of projects you could do if you were working. This is your passion. You have found a way to make the world brighter and a better place.

2. Make sure you are self-motivated. To be in business, any business, you have to be self-motivated. You may be extremely creative using your Cricut, but if you are not motivated to network and get customers consistently, that's going to be a problem in the long run. Also, you might have to work on projects when you don't feel like working because

people need their purchases. Are you motivated enough to be able to keep up the pace a business sometimes throws your way? Also, are you ready to deal with "that" customer? We are talking about the customer who just is never happy. You need a plan for the bad penny that just will not go away.

3. Make sure your personal finances are in order. And then consult with an advisor and an accountant before going into business and take their advice. Make sure according to the financial advisors you can weather any storms that come along because of low tides in the business world. You don't want to ruin your love for your Cricut by ending up in financial trouble because you were not financially prepared to go into business in the first place. There is truly nothing worse than thinking you have found your dream and ending up in a daytime nightmare.

4. A good question to ask yourself is where will I get my clients? Etsy? Pinterest? Word of Mouth? Will you market on Facebook? How are you going to get your customers? Are you planning to go to craft fairs? Think about your options and what marketing is going to cost. Are you ready to beat the pavement? Go to schools, churches, hit up the little leagues and everyone and anyone who needs something done by a Cricut?

5. Everyone who goes into business should have a solid business plan. A business plan is a road map of where you are and where you are going. How much things might potentially cost and the potential income. With a Cricut Maker, you don't have as many outside variables and most of the success depends on your hard work and persistence. But you still need a business plan and a good one! Let's get started!

Once these five steps have been addressed, you are ready to get started with your new Cricut Maker Business. How exciting!

You need a Business Name and a Logo

Now that you know your machine, and you have decided to take the plunge into owning your own business with your Cricut, you need to think of a name for this business and a symbol of you. Your name for your business needs to identify you and also be a catchy name that tells people what you do. Pick a name you plan to stick with for a long time. It's costly to change a name and logo, etc. A logo isn't necessary, but they are fun to design and you have a Cricut Maker, so play around with your new name and design.

What Kind of a Business License Will You Need?

One of the steps you will have to do is to contact your home state because every state is different in how to obtain a state business license. A **license** or **permit** gives you the permission you need to open and operate a business. A **registration** allows you to claim the name of the business and the business itself as yours. **Insurance** is another matter and is usually not mandatory with a crating business, but it does cover costs in case of an accident.

Your business probably will, according to state law, need a **license** to operate legally; even if you are operating a small sole proprietorship and running this business out of your home. This is something you need to investigate immediately and get those details in order first. An accountant or financial advisor will be able to help you. Usually these people are able to help for a minimal charge or do not mind answering questions for free.

You can also go to your city or county business office and ask questions. Often, there are people there who can answer questions and even help you fill out the necessary paperwork. If your state capital is not far, you could do the same by going to the licensing division at your state capital.

Also, consult with other people who are in the crafting business. Note, we said consult. This does not mean to take everything they say as the law. You still need to check the laws in your own county and state, but at least if you check with others in the crafting business before you take the plunge, you will have an idea of the cost and paperwork.

And speaking of taking the plunge, are you ready to jump right in or is this going to be a part-time gig for a while to see how you do? Most people do start part-time. Again, talk to others and get some ideas. No one can choose for you, but this is one business you could do part-time for a while in the evenings and on weekends before you quit your day job. These things are all important discussions to have before you decide what to do about getting into business using your Cricut Maker on a full-time basis.

Website

The next order of business is to work on a website. You will need to find a host. Many people like Bluehost. And, while you are at it, print yourself some business cards on your Cricut. How fun is it to design and print your own cards on your Cricut Maker?

Business cards are important because they are your own little billboard. They are a way to advertise every time you give one out or pin one on a bulletin board in a restaurant or a coffee shop. Your phone number is on the card and an idea of what you will create for your customers is on your card. You also will put your business email address on your business cards.

Business Facebook

You should also set up a business Facebook page. A business Facebook page is a fun and profitable page to set up. Facebook actually guides you through a step by step process to help make this easy and effortless. This is a great way to network with friends and then to boost posts for a small fee to target potential clients who might be interested in purchasing what you are making with your Cricut Maker. You can easily see posts and messages on all accounts when you log onto FB with your personal or business account. You can then link things to make to this business FB page and boost those things out. This is perfect for seasonal crafts, Back to School, Wedding niches. Whatever your niche is, you can find a way to market your products on FB and then boost them out to people who are ready to buy what you are selling.

Choosing a Niche

Do you have a niche? Are you best at printing T-shirts? Or printing vinyl on dishes? Maybe you want to market printing on canvas bags. Recently, this author's daughter just ordered 100 canvas bags for her church, from a Cricut crafter who prints vinyl for a living. She charged $12.00 a bag. I'm sure her profit is about $10.00 each. This is one order from one small church. This particular crafter has a niche and is making a great profit and keeping her prices competitive with other similar products in the same niche.

Think of how many churches there are in your community? What if you took a business card with a flyer stapled to it and a picture of a sample canvas bag of a church on the flyer. How many orders do you think you might get from just a little bit of marketing hustle? If just 20 churches out of 50 ordered canvas bags and they each ordered 100 bags. Do the math. So that's 2000 bags with a profit of $10.00 per bag. That comes to $20,000. I don't do this for a living, but I assume the more bags you buy in bulk, the cheaper they become. This is what we are talking about when we say to choose a niche. A person could make a good living just printing canvas bags. We only gave a church example. Think of schools, dance clubs, girl scouts and shopping. Canvas bags we can use over and over are a green way to go!

Another piece of advice when working with products for selling is to keep your products competitive with other products similar to yours but be wary of undercutting everyone. Your profit margin will not be enough to justify the work you are doing. A smart business plan is paying you per the hour you are working. At least eventually, you should earn a wage. You will not do that by undercutting everyone else. On the flip side of this coin, if your prices are too high, people will not buy what you are selling either. That defeats the entire purpose of being in business with your Cricut.

Where and what you sell will be determined by your state as to what kind of business license you need.

Finances

Your Cricut business should be able to buy your materials and pay your wage for your work. Somewhere in your business plan you should have the initial cost of your Cricut Maker and accessories. Plan to recover those costs as repayment to you. This should be a loan repayment line item in your budget. An accountant should be able to help with this. If you have any online fees, etc., those are also to be paid by your business or reimbursed if you do not have a separate account. Please get a separate business account as soon as you are able. This will also keep things from becoming confusing for your accountant and will keep taxes from becoming a nightmare at the end of the year.

How do you Plan to Sell Items and Get Orders?

Are you planning to sell items on Etsy? Will you market on Pinterest, do craft shows, Tweet, Facebook boost your business posts, or get the word out another way? A good idea is to try a different strategy every month. Put this in your business plan. Maybe have a list of craft shows or get your products in a few places that do consignment only. You can take your Cricut and make products on the spot. Maybe host a Cricut party. Let people choose things for you to make for them. Take orders of personalized outfits for their grandkids. Grandparents love to buy personalized shirts and outfits.

Tennis shoes and hats are another big Cricut marketing option when you go into business. The nice feature of Design Space is that the trademark of many items has been purchased through Cricut so you can print some logos and designs you would not be able to use otherwise with another vinyl printer. That said, do not use anyone else's work or trademark if it is not legally purchased by Cricut. You cannot use Disney if Cricut does not have Disney. Or you cannot use Coca Cola, for instance. Please, please do not sell what someone else has designed. You probably will hear from their lawyers. Even if you are small, you will get a letter and you might be prosecuted. Just don't do it.

Strategies

The strategies for marketing and selling your items is part of the fun of owning your own Cricut Maker business. Brainstorm and you will be able to come up with at least one option for each month and many of these options will carry over from month to month. For instance, craft shows are abundant in the fall. Etsy is ongoing. A drawback of Etsy is there is a cost, but many people swear by Etsy. You can market your Etsy site through Pinterest and even Facebook and Twitter. However, don't bite off more than you can chew. Try one at a time and master one at a time. Don't push yourself beyond your comfort zone. Even though you are in business, this is still supposed to be fun!

Previously, it was mentioned to begin a website. On your website, once you get comfortable, it is a nice idea to start a blog about your Cricut Maker and the projects that are fun to try. Build interest in what you do. There are some crafters who end up having so many affiliate sponsors they make more money from the sponsors than they do with their products. Post videos and take pictures of your products. Other Cricut Maker users want to learn from you. Be a leader and a teacher in your field. Answer questions. Be informative.

Taking Orders

Make sure when you take an order, you are able to complete the order by the time you say you can complete the order. There isn't anything that hurts your reputation more than letting a customer down. That said, if you are going to be delayed, you have to communicate early. However, if this customer needs 20 T-shirts for the first ball game on June 1 and you said you would have those shirts ready by May 15. You need to get those shirts ready. Or by April 15, let the customer know. Do you understand the timeliness and why it's so important for certain items? The printing business does have deadlines. People need things for Christmas and other holidays. Please do not commit to what you cannot deliver. And check your spelling two and three times. There is only one thing worse than a late order, and that is an order that is on time and is completely wrong. If you are stumped about fonts and where to go, there is another site called Dafont.com. This might help with customers, and what they may be looking for when they order.

Recently a person was contacted on Pinterest about her Cricut business. She immediately sent an email and then a free gift of a pattern for a Cricut craft to the person who inquired. In fact, 5 very nice emails have been sent over the course of 3 days. Not pushy, just informative. This is how to market a Cricut business, friends. This is how it is done.

Honestly, most of the emails are probably sent out automatically for efficiency unless there is a reply, but what great service to a potential client! Marketing your website and also yourself and your niche all are found in what this Cricut user is doing. She is teaching, networking, and being a friend to newbies.

Possible Products to Sell

The possibilities are endless of the projects you can create and sell with your Cricut Maker, so let's focus on a few hot items people sell online and at craft fairs.

Canvas Wall Art

The way to make Canvas Wall Art using your Cricut Maker is to buy a blank canvas.

The canvas might be as big or small as you want your design to be.

Choose a quote or design.

Make stencils out of the designs and use those stencils to create lovely and meaningful canvas art

Personalized Tools

Cut vinyl lettering with your Cricut Maker and place on hammers for instance. Great gift ideas for Mother's Day and Father's Day.

Wedding Specialties

People earn a living with their Cricut Making working on personalized Bride and Groom accessories and wedding party accessories for weddings and engagements. Weddings are a big business and they happen year-round. The income from wedding projects ranges from water bottles, to invitations, place cards, programs, bridesmaid robes, champagne glasses, his and hers glasses, mugs, koozies and more! The list could be endless for this particular niche.

A perfect idea would be to team up with a wedding coordinator or popular venue and share business back and forth. They do this all the time with caterers, bartenders, and security professionals. Get out there and network what you are able to do in your business.

As with any business, again, marketing and business sense is important. As stated before, a very creative individual will not last in business if they cannot get the word out about how good their work is and attract new customers to buy their products. By the same token, if you are not following a business plan, and charge too little for services or products, you may run yourself out of business. Also, keep in close contact with an accountant and keep personal money from business money.

Just a quick interjection about business as a reminder. You cannot be reminded too often in this section that running a business is fun because you are using your Cricut Maker, but running a business is also work and requires a person to take some time each day to manage the work of the business.

Kitchen Gadgets

Kitchen supplies and gadgets such as coffee cups, cutting boards and so much more can have fun sayings written on them in vinyl lettering. People love personalized items in their kitchen. Word of mouth spreads fast for these types of products. Making personalized kitchen gadgets a few months before Christmas is a good idea as orders will likely come in quickly once people learn what you are able to do. And while you are personalizing kitchen items, try personalizing kitchen towels as well. People love colorful kitchen towels made just for them or with whimsical sayings on them.

T-Shirts

You can create a business around selling personalized clothing, especially if you are willing to market. If I were doing a clothing business with the Cricut, I would make sure every youth sports league and adult league had flyers about my Cricut business for printing uniform shirts, hats, etc... then I would continue to market on Facebook and have a Pinterest board set up as well as an Etsy shop ready for orders.

I would also market to every grandmother in the city about buying "I'm Two Years Old" shirts, and "I'm Five Years Old." You get the idea. Get the word out and more printing orders will come in than you can handle.

Your Cricut Business in Summary

There are so many more projects you can make and sell with your Cricut Maker. What separates a successful businessperson who is able to sell crafts that he or she makes from one who cannot, is the knowledge and the marketing side of the business. If you are good at using your Cricut Maker and you have a niche that you feel you could be the number one seller in the marker, jump in! Dot your I's and cross those t's. You will be glad you took the time to do this business correctly and run this as a business.

Yes, you love doing crafts and you love your Cricut Maker and helping people to be happy and satisfied with your products. But you also know, the "business" side of the business has to be covered. And then, you will truly love what you do for a living and do what you love!

Chapter 9

Extending the life of your machine and when to know if you need an upgrade

Your Cricut Maker is amazing and there is no doubt about it. But as amazing as this machine is, there is going to be some wear and tear and you will need to do some troubleshooting from time to time. Just like computers are to techies, when these wonderful machines work, they are the best thing since sliced bread for crafters to own. However, when they have a glitch or a malfunction, an otherwise benevolent crafter may want to throw his or her Cricut Maker right out the window.

But please, refrain, for most of the minor problems just take a little bit of patience and knowhow to get you back up and running again into your next project. And, most fixes are simple and quick fixes with very little effort.

Let's take these minor problems one at a time and see if we can solve some troubleshooting with some easy and painless solutions.

1. **The material is tearing when it is trying to cut.**
   When this happens, it is possible that the mat is not

sticky enough to hold the material in place. You might be using the incorrect mat or the stickiness has worn off. Use the green mat for the material. Remember, the blue mat is for paper and the purple mat is for really heavy material such as leather. There might be other reasons why the material is slipping. They include:

- You need to adjust your cutting settings
- The blade should be replaced
- The blade may be the incorrect blade for the job.
- Lastly, the material might not be compatible with the Cricut Maker. This rarely happens, but once in a blue moon it does. More often with the older machines you might find this. Not so much with the Cricket Maker.

2. **The transfer tape isn't working.** Transfer tape may take some time to get used to. You should watch some videos. There are plenty on several Pinterest sites and Cricut videos as well of how to do every step with the Cricut Maker. However, when you are trying to use transfer tape and it doesn't come up when you want it to, this is one of those moments that can test a person's patience. Glitter vinyl seems to be the hardest to transfer. Regular transfer tape does not work well with the glitter vinyl for some reason. For the glitter, use Cricut brand StrongGrip

transfer tape. But most vinyls come with their own tape or just use regular transfer tape.

3. The blade is cutting all the way through the material. Again, this is super frustrating.
- Make sure the blade is clear if you can spray it with compressed air.
- Make sure the blade is pressed in all the way.
- Check to see if your Cricut is on the correct setting for the material you are cutting. A suggestion is to always use a test cut. This should help.

4. Sometimes images do not show up on the mat. You might have an image correctly set and it lines up perfectly in Design Space but looks completely wonky or doesn't show up at all on the mat when you begin to cut. The easy fix is to press "group" and then "attach" all the layers panel before you cut. Then they will stay just where you want them to stay.

Should I Buy a Used Cricut?

There are times when we have to solve little glitches, but more times than not, these are small things like the examples above. The question has come up about buying a used Cricut Maker and is this a cost-effective purchase?

Would there be more troubleshooting involved from a used machine?

Let's begin by first looking at the age of machine you buy in the first place when you purchase a Cricut Maker. How used is the machine? Or are you going to buy a slightly used machine. After learning about the Cricut Maker and doing extensive research on the machine and how to use the Cricut maker to make various projects, one has to guess, there might be people who buy a Cricut Maker and then perhaps only use it slightly. I would not recommend buying a really worn out machine.

If a Cricut Maker was barely used and available for a substantially less price, buying a used Cricut Maker might be worth the gamble. The only drawback of buying a used machine is you might not get some of the free addons and programs you get when you buy and new machine. You will have to inquire from the person you buy a used machine from at the time you ask questions before purchase. This is important.

There are also discounts and coupons from Cricut, JoAnn's and Michael's at different times. Watch for these sales when thinking about your purchase.

How to help Your Cricut Maker Run in Top Condition Longer

Keep your machine clean and run your machine according to instructions. Make sure to use the correct blades for cutting the weight of materials. Use the blades needed for heavier materials.

Keep your software updated. Instructions are included with your Cricut Maker.

You can always contact the company:

US/CA: 877-7CRICUT
UK: 0808 101 7032
AU: 1800953076
NZ: 0800463844
Other: +1 801 937 9075

Chapter 10

Definitions Associated with the Cricut Maker

There are several words that are uniquely associated with the Cricut Maker and then there are some words that mean something completely different than the usual meaning when used in conjunction with your Cricut Maker. Because of this, we thought adding a Definitions chapter was important to this Guide. For example, the word "attach" is a tool in our definitions, but Webster defines this different. The word makes sense as you do use the attach tool to keep things in place, but the definition is not what you would expect "attach" to be. This is why we created the definitions section:

Attach – The attach tool is located in Design Space. If you decide to purchase Design Space, you will use the attach tool. This is the tool that helps to hold your cuts in place on your cutting mat in the design screen. It also helps to fasten a score layer to cut a layer after you score it.

Contour – The contour tool is also a feature you can use in Design Space. As this guide has demonstrated, Design Space is used often. Contour removes unwanted cut lines and is therefore very useful for beginners, especially.

Compound Path – This is a term used to define when all the cut lines are grouped together. You can also edit the compound lines by grouping the compound paths together and the right-click to release the compound path.

Cut Lines – This is the same term that is used with a basic sewing pattern and the symbol scissors is marked on the pattern. The cut lines are where the shape is supposed to be cut. These lines are either red or gray and this is where your Cricut Make will cut whatever it is you are cutting. These lines are also where your pens will draw if you are drawing or writing.

Decal - A decal is the product you have after you finish cutting shapes from vinyl.

Design Space – This is the program your guide has been talking so much about. There are many projects and fonts you can access in Design Space. Design Space is pretty necessary for the Cricut Maker to do everything it needs to do.

Firmware – Firmware is a program that is already on your Cricut Maker. Updates will occur when you plug your Cricut Maker into your laptop.

Floating Panels – These panels are used so you can work in different areas at the same time. You can cut in one area while designing in another.

Force – Force is the amount of pressure you apply with the blade to the thickness of the material you are using. This ensures a complete and sharp cut regardless of how thick the material might be.

Group/Ungroup – To group or Ungroup is a command that helps you to do just what this action says it does. You are able to combine several layers or images together. This even allows you to combine multiple layers of text together. In reverse action, this command allows you to ungroup a set of layers or images. They will then be able to move independently of each other.

Heat Transfer Vinyl – Remember when you had to have numbers or letters put on the back of shirts by an outside company? With a Cricut Maker, you are able to use a specialty vinyl that can be used on fabrics to create those designs. This vinyl comes with an adhesive backing and a sheet so it can be cut just right to fit on the fabric.

Kiss cut – Kiss cut is a very precise cut made that only cuts through one layer. It is a thin top layer usually cut when making a decal.

Mirrored Image – A mirrored image is the reverse of any image. Most of the iron-on materials have to be mirrored. The software will tell you when to turn on the mirror image tool. This is used in Design Space and is something you use before doing your cuts.

Offset – Often when people think of offset, they think of an offset press as in printing. This is much like a printing press function. You choose the distance you want around the border of any design. It can be a predesign or a design of your own. The offset function is used often in sign making.

Print then Cut – The print then cut feature is what allows you to print from your computer to your home printer. Then the Cricut can die cut the design.

Printable Vinyl – Printable vinyl is vinyl that can be sent through the home printer and then the Cricut is able to die cut it. It is also called a print and cut function.

Reverse Weeding – Reverse weeding is when you remove vinyl that is left behind after you make stencils or other cuts.

Scraper – The scraper is sometimes called a squeegee. This is a flat tool that is used to smoothen out transfer tape and other thin material like decals.

Sketching – Sketching is the same thing as drawing, only this action is done by your machine with any of the pens. You can use the pen included with the machine or buy extra pens from Cricut or use pens from any pen section. Some will work better than others. Just experiment with this fun activity.

Slice – The slice action and tool create a new path from two images. This will result in completely new images or shapes. They should show up in the layers panel as individual layers.

Spatula – You will use a spatula often once you are more familiar with the Cricut Maker. This is a tool used to remove smaller pieces of vinyl or paper from mats after you have made cuts

SVG – SVG files are files that are used in the Cricut Maker. These are traced images that can be made larger or smaller and they do not lose resolution.

Teflon – Teflon is a thin waxy sheet that is used when ironing. This Teflon is used to protect your iron or your heat press. Just like the Teflon on a pan, this sturdy, but thin material stands up to heat and makes it possible for you do use heat for your projects.

Text to Path – When you do text to path, this is an action of moving the text to curve it around a pattern or a shape like a square or a circle.

Transfer Tape – Transfer tape is a special tape that is used to move adhesive vinyl from the carrier sheet to the surface of whatever kind of project you are working on.

Weeding – When you are weeding, think of the process you used in your garden, only transfer that to removing unwanted vinyl from a decal.

Weeding lines – Weeding lines are the cut lines that make it easier to cut out a project, aka, weeding.

Weld – The weld tool allows you to join shapes to create a single object.

ZIP File – A ZIP file is a compressed or smaller-sized file containing one or more files. You will need to unzip the file to get access to the contents by right-clicking the ZIP and clicking "Extract all...". macOS users can unzip a zip file by double-clicking the file or moving it to the desktop and then double-clicking the file.

Conclusion

The purpose of this guide is not to sell Cricut Makers, but rather to help people who are using Cricut Makers become more familiar with their machine and become more satisfied with their crafting tool. However, even though this guide was not created to sell Cricut Makers, two Cricut Makers have been purchased during the production of this guide! The Cricut maker is life changing. A good one-word description is "amazing." From a crafter's point of view, there is so much a Cricut Maker helps a crafter create. The interesting feature is that the more a person is into crafting, the more this person will use their Cricut Maker and the more a person uses their Cricut Maker, the more they will work on crafting projects. It's a continuing cycle for someone who loves to create fun crafts and gifts.

Every single holiday is enhanced by decorations that can be made using the Cricut Maker. And every birthday, or any other occasion, is enhanced by personalized gifts that can be created using the Cricut Maker. Mother's Days and Father's Days will never be the same now that you have a new Cricut Maker! Every vacation your family will enjoy matching shirts to celebrate the occasion. Your youngest munchkin is turning 2? Bam! T-Shirt done for the 2nd-year-old's birthday party! Do you have a wedding or anniversary? His and Her cups are on the way!

The Cricut Maker literally changes everything about gift-giving and decorating around the house. You will not have to buy any more canvas prints of whimsical or wise sayings because you can cut and print your own. People will want to know where you are getting your new décor and will remark at the clean lines of your latest stylish personalized dishes.

The only way to get the full impact of what your Cricut can do is to get the machine out and use it. Digging in and getting started is the best way to get familiar with your new Cricut Maker. There are several projects you can start right away. Be sure to check the materials needed and get those ready before you begin. If you haven't read this full Guide, make sure you do that. We have several tips for you to help make learning about your Cricut Maker more efficient.

The temptation to run your own business is strong. And why not? People are already asking you to make things. You might as well think strongly about opening your own shop with your Cricut. You can specialize in any number of products. Remember, the key is to find your niche and then market your product and yourself in a variety of ways. The key is to make sure you are enjoying what you do and making more than you spend. Who knows? This could be an income stream that pays the bills at some point. There are plenty of Cricut users on Pinterest and Etsy who do just that!

With your Cricut Maker, you can actually make hundreds, even thousands of projects. The ideas are endless. We could not begin to list them all in this Cricut Maker Guide. We did give you several to try, but the rest is for you to research and explore. You should have gotten 50 project instructions with your new Cricut Maker. And these are just the tip of the iceberg!

This guide also gave you several projects to try and a list of simple materials you need for each so you know exactly what you need for each craft. The Guide also has a comprehensive list of accessories and what each accessory is able to do to enhance your Cricut Maker experience. We have listed some sewing projects to get you started with sewing as well.

You should understand how to set your Cricut Maker up when you read the beginning of this guide. We cannot stress enough, watching videos that are available. Cricut has several available as well as many on YouTube and Pinterest. There is literally a community of Cricut Maker friends online right now ready to welcome you as a new Cricut Maker user. Be a little careful. Some of them are trying to make a living and they are selling things. Most of what you need is free. Accessories are always available for a cost. Be a choosy spender and save your money for some of the accessories that you actually do need to go with your Cricut Maker.

Speaking of accessories, yes, Cricut Access is worth the price and necessary to have. But there are other accessories you need as well as outlined in this guide. Remember, there are coupons from places like JoAnn's and Michael's to help save money on different things you want and need. The key is finding the accessories for the price you can afford for when you need them.

The Cricut Maker is a fun machine that can also be a way to earn some cash. Business aside, the Cricut Maker is revolutionary in the crafting and sewing world. With its new rotary blade, this machine is the first of its kind to cut through different materials like it does. And the writing tools make this the writing machine able to write like never before. You can literally change any design to look like a drawing and the Cricut writer will draw and add the different colors to the drawing. The machine will tell you when to change pens and which colors to use. Or, you can use the pen color that will best resemble a pencil drawing for that effect.

The drawing option is another tool that will help add a special feature to a wall hanging, crafting project, or to another sewing project. There is literally no limit as to what this tool can do.

This drawing tool is also available to do the usual addressing of envelopes, designing letters, cards, and crafting of special lettering of specialty signs. With all the fonts available, you can have fun experimenting on paper and enjoying learning the many different ways to use these things.

Bottom line, the Cricut Maker is going to change the way you do most of your crafting and decorating. With all the ideas available in crafting, sewing, quilting, etching, and writing, this new Cricut Maker is the machine to turn your crafting room into a wealth of new projects.

Made in the
USA
Monee, IL

15891971R00081